# ORIGINS OF THE TRANSATLANTIC POLICY
## OF DEMOCRATIC REPUBLIC OF CONGO

The *Droit / Économie international* collection contains the works of authors who are specialists in the fields of law and economics and was created to give a better understanding and knowledge of the topical issues raised by the evolution and globalisation of markets.

Edited by:
Bernard REMICHE, *lawyer and professor at the Université catholique de Louvain, Director of the Arcelor Chair, former President of the Association internationale de Droit économique, Belgium.*
Nicolas THIRION, *professor at the Université de Liège, Director of the Legal Theory and Commercial Law Unit of the Faculty of Law.*

## In the same collection: :

# ORIGINS OF THE TRANSATLANTIC POLICY OF DEMOCRATIC REPUBLIC OF CONGO

## Democratic Republic of Congo, Land of hope for humanity

Vital Kamerhe

Preface by Michel Rocard

Foreword by
Grégoire Bakandeja wa Mpungu

Droit | Économie international

 larcier

For any information on our collections and the latest additions in your own specialist field, visit our website: www.larcier.com

© Group De Boeck s.a., 2012
Éditions Larcier
Rue des Minimes, 39 • B-1000 Brussels, Belgium

Printed in Belgium

Legal registration 2012/0031/091                    ISBN : 978-2-8044-4797-7

*To my late father, Constantin Kamerhe,*
*and my mother, Mwankingi Alphonsine,*
*who watched over me from my first steps*
*to the end of my university studies.*

*To my wife, Mamick, and my children.*

*To Congolese and African people.*

# Contents

PART TWO
**DRC: ECONOMIC POTENTIAL CONTRASTED WITH LEVEL
OF DEVELOPMENT AND REALISTIC EXPECTATIONS**

# Acknowledgements

As this book is the result of a combined effort, I hesitated for a while before venturing upon the difficult task of acknowledgements for fear of forgetting some people who might have made a significant contribution to its writing.

I already apologise to whoever might have been omitted for lack of attention on my part.

I owe a debt of gratitude to Mr Michel ROCARD, former French Prime Minister, this grand man of science, a prominent figure in French and European politics and whose intelligence and political experience has had a great deal of impact on me since my university days. Without any doubt for economists like myself, he ranks very high among those politicians who have managed to balance science with government through his pragmatic approach towards economics. I found him very fascinating and could hardly have imagined that our paths would ever cross.

I thank him most sincerely for the honour he has bestowed on me in writing the preface to this book.

By inviting me to the cycle of conferences organised by his centre every year, and by suggesting that I focus on the subject of "Reconsidering the Atlantic", Professor Dorval BRUNELLE, Director of the Institute for International Studies at the University of Quebec in Montreal (IQAM) gave me the opportunity to express my ideas on the substantial role that the Democratic Republic of Congo must play in Africa, in the Atlantic area, and why not worldwide, given its tremendous natural resources which can offer a significant response to the major challenges confronting mankind.

Monsieur Bernard DE ROME, President of the same institute, and a renowned journalist with Radio Canada, had very kindly agreed to play his part, so competently, in my conference at the UQAM amphitheatre on 17 February 2010. The relevance of the questions he raised enabled me to reconsider some sections of this book so that I could, as far as possible, reconsider some of the concerns expressed on this occasion. Through him, I would like to thank the television and Radio Canada for covering this event and whose images and recordings stimulated a response in my own country and worldwide, which I incorporated in my research.

Following on from Professor BRUNELLE, the Vice-Rector of the University had been so kind as to introduce the subject of the day and outline what the academic body could expect from my speech.

I also appreciated the solidarity and contribution of my compatriots in Canada who, by their constructive and unpretentious criticism, helped me to gain a better understanding of the economic impetus of the Democratic Republic of Congo (DRC) in the current context of globalisation.

I would be failing at this stage if I did not give credit to the support of the Congolese professors and other Africans at the University of Ottawa who, despite their numerous academic duties, unhesitatingly accepted to have a debate with me during an academic conference on the issue of African development and who shared my vision of the role of my country, DRC.

In this same context, I would like to thank the Rector and the academic authorities of the Université Laval in Quebec City and the University of Ottawa for giving me a platform in their prestigious institutions.

I do not want to omit other Canadian authorities and institutions with which I have had a rewarding exchange of views on the future of DRC and on other matters of common interest in the Triatlantic zone. I am particularly thinking of the President of the House of Commons, the President of the Canada-Africa Friendship Group, the Honourable Mauril BÉLANGER, and all the Members and Senators who accompanied him, the top people at the Ministry of Foreign Affairs and other federal bodies, the Deputy Mayor of the City of Montreal and Honorary President of the House of Commons, the Board of the Missionary Mutual Aid Society for its continuing interest in DRC.

I should also like to thank Madame Syndrid JOHNSSON, The Canadian Ambassador in DRC, for all the facilities and vital documentation made available to me.

2

This book has been enriched with considerable assistance from professors with different standpoints. Hence, I should like to thank all those who, through their research, their knowledge, experience and availability made a contribution to the final book. They are primarily Professors Sayeman BULA BULA, Jean-Pierre MAVUNGU et BIYOYA, professors at the University of Kinshasa, Mr Liévin CHIRLHALWIRWA, Professor at the Polytechnic and Building Institute in Kinshasa, as well as Mr Floribert NYAMOYA.

Moreover, I should like to pay tribute to the work carried out by Mr Grégoire BAKANDEJA, Honorary Dean and Professor at the Universities of Kinshasa and Paris I Sorbonne, Mr Kadari MWENE KABYANA, Professor at the University of Quebec in Chicoutimi and Mr Bernard REMICHE, Professor at the Université Catholique de Louvain.

They all agreed to correct, review and revise the text of this book.

I cannot remain silent about the scientific contribution of Mr Joseph MUKUMBU, Mr Sam SANGAMAYI, Fathers Jean Bosco BAHALA and Rigobert MINANI, and also Mr Louis MUMBALA BOM, DRC Chargé d'affaires in Brazil.

I would also like to thank my fellow Members of Parliament, Élysée DIMANDJA, Justin BITAKWIRA, Fidel TINGOMBAYI and Aimé BOJI SANGARA, who also contributed to this work with their scientific and practical knowledge.

I wish to express my heartfelt gratitude to my colleagues for their constant availability and who took great care to ensure the quality of the final book. Their names are Pierre KANGUDIA MBAYI, Jean-Baudoin MYO MAMBEKE, Saturnin ZIRIMANI, Willy KALENGAY, Jean-Marie BAMPORIKI, Placide KAMANZI, Richie MUHOZI, Thierry CACI CIZUNGU, Kaiko MAKOLO, Christian LANGU, Jean-Jacques TAMFURI and Eddy BAKANA.

Finally, I should like to thank those heads of government departments who were patriotic enough to let me have the statistical data and publications I needed. They include the Ministry for the Environment and Nature Preservation, the Ministries of Energy, Agriculture, Mines, Hydrocarbons, for National Defence and the Central Bank of Congo.

# Preface

Conducting a triangular study on the relationships between States sharing the Atlantic Ocean, means asking questions without expecting an immediate answer, but also means placing oneself inside a future framework with roots going back in time.

The approach is interesting and more than just a topic from the current era of economic and financial internationalisation and globalisation. It is inherently likely to stimulate intellectual debates which must lead to fresh solutions to the great contemporary challenges.

In fact and though not very new, the subject of this book, the *Origins of the Transatlantic Policy of the Democratic Republic of Congo*, is innovative because it deals with an African country with a natural vocation to play an important role in the latest transatlantic relationships founded on complementarity and solidarity.

More than a vision, this is a willingness, an action plan from a Congolese politician, who is very dynamic and enterprising, and whose deep-rooted conviction is to make the Congo once again a prosperous and powerful country at the heart of the African continent; a legitimate ambition for any open-minded nationalist but which, according to the author, is achievable given the considerable advantages and opportunities to be had in this country. For the author, Mr Vital KAMERHE, ex-President of the National Assembly in his country, this is more than just a conviction. Through his invitation to preface this book, which I was pleased to accept, Mr KAMERHE encourages me to share with him ambitious ideas for the Democratic Republic of Congo and the entire African Continent.

My encounter with Vital KAMERHE occurred during a visit paid to Kinshasa in September 2008 to attend the first international conference of the Institut Euro-africain de Droit Economique (Euro-African Institute for Economic Law), INEADEC. During our meeting (arranged by Professors Bernard REMICHE and Grégoire BAKANDEJA) outside the conference proper, I appreciated his quick mind and his clear-sighted ideas on the future of his country and the role he would like it to play on the international stage, and in Africa in particular.

This book is the reflection of a vision for the Congo, founded on commitment. It is based on the hope of seeing the Democratic Republic of the Congo get back on track, no longer appearing with a beggar's bowl when it possesses many advantages, both natural and human which should allow it to become a driving force for sustainable development on the entire African Continent.

Yes, the Democratic Republic of Congo is the "dream paradise on earth", rich in natural resources, water, forests, fauna and flora) but also with an abundance of mining resources (copper, cobalt, iron, manganese, gold, diamonds, coltan, phosphate, oil, natural gas, etc.) stimulating, however, the greed of companies with few scruples and often not very respectful of the legitimate interests of local people. It also possesses substantial human resources.

So many assets and opportunities, which, if well-managed, will enable it to play a major role on the world stage.

Hence, taking his inspiration from the model of Brazil, the Latin American country which has achieved an unprecedented economic impetus so that it is now ranked alongside the great developing countries; Vital KAMERHE is convinced that with an unfailing political will and with an efficient political organization, mindful of the people's future, the Congo's resources may also make it an emerging country, bringing a sustainable development to its inhabitants and worldwide opportunities.

This book also includes interesting thoughts about nationalist sentiments, especially in the Congo, and includes a lucid and courageous analysis of the causes of the "Congolese sickness".

For all these reasons and many more, I have no doubt that this book will be useful for any debate on the future of Congo, Africa and the Atlantic relationships.

So I wish him a long and rewarding career.

*Paris,*

Michel ROCARD

Former Prime Minister

6

# Foreword

For some twenty years, there has been talk of a multifaceted crisis (economic, social and political) in the Democratic Republic of Congo (DRC). In reality, this is a human and system crisis; a situation which for man, society and government, reflects a record of errors from the past and calls for a thorough examination and reforms for a change of direction. But the population expects the politicians to bring practical solutions to improve the situation.

This book is a study conducted by a prominent political figure who lived and lives in an administrative system that he intends to challenge so as to take advantage of the assets and opportunities available in his country to satisfy the expectations of its population and the rest of the world.

Fascinated by a proven model of development in the Latin American country of Brazil, the author makes the analogy to demonstrate that with the same assets as this country (natural, mining, agricultural and human resources), Congo can and must develop and contribute to the development of mankind.

As is well known, DRC is a country that, ever since 1996, has been confronted with a long war, which some have described as an African World War, and by insecurity up to the end of 2004. This situation has caused the country a considerable delay in terms of growth and development. The Congo has declined to such a point that it is classified today amongst the poor countries which form the category of Least Developed Countries, according to United Nations' criteria.

In such a situation, it was a matter of urgency that its sons and daughters should ask questions about the dramatic fate in store for a country endowed with so many attributes to play a decisive role in the hall of nations. Hence their questioning of the drama that the population is experiencing and their misgivings about the politicians as well as the Congolese intelligentsia.

This book makes an attempt to respond to some of these doubts and suggests some ways forward to provide solutions as well as adequate means to gradually get the country out of the abyss into which it has sunk. Refusing to be a fatalist, the author rejects this image of a poor country and uses Brazil as a model of a South Atlantic country with striking similarities to DRC, in order to make plans for Congo to become prosperous and powerful in the near future, purged of the bad economic administration and all those worthless values preventing its economic take-off. A revitalised Congo which will make use of its own resources before calling for help from outside partnerships. And as a convincing argument, the author uses Brazil as an example, a country where similar political, economic and social problems have been experienced and resolved by the volition of its leaders. As a reminder, the Brazilians created the ways and means in advance so that they could count upon their own efforts before appealing to multilateral financial donors. There were times when they broke ties with these multilateral donors, but they have now been welcomed back into the international financial community. To achieve these positive results, they abolished bad administrative practices and the wrongs eating their way into the social order (dictatorship, corruption, poverty and racism). In so doing, they created the conditions where they could emerge as a respected economic power on the world stage.

In order to believe in a better future where Congo is prosperous and developed in the image of Brazil, the author insists on one condition, an efficient and efficacious economic system and the creation of a State with democratic laws.

Without pointing a finger at whoever is responsible for the present national drama (the worsening of poverty, misery and its social consequences) who seems to take delight in international begging, the author sounds a warning bell for a real change in economic management methods currently marked by the predatory nature and prevarication at the top level of public authority, so that shameful instances of corruption and misappropriation can be halted. He is suggesting plans to make Congo not just a real paradise for its inhabitants but also and especially an opportunity for the whole world. He has this conviction and belief. This belief is based upon the capacity of DRC to be innovative and technologically advanced, making use of its important human values, the dynamism of its population and particularly its young people, the immeasurable riches of its environment and the abundance of its resources above and under the ground.

These ideas are covered in detail in the three sections that make up this book, followed by the bibliography.

Finally, it is to be hoped that this book will stimulate debate nurtured by intellectual and practical considerations, based upon a vision of an attainable development, in the context of a three-cornered America – Europe – Africa alliance.

Grégoire BAKANDEJA wa MPUNGU

PhD in economic law (France)

University Professor

(at the Universities of Kinshasa and Sorbonne, Paris I)

Honorary Dean

# Geographical maps

Map of the administrative areas of the Democratic Republic of the
Congo and the bordering States which comprise the Congo Basin

*Source: http://maps.mygeo.info/cont/cartes/2007/Carte_Republique_
democratique_du_Congo_2007.gif.*

## Map of Africa

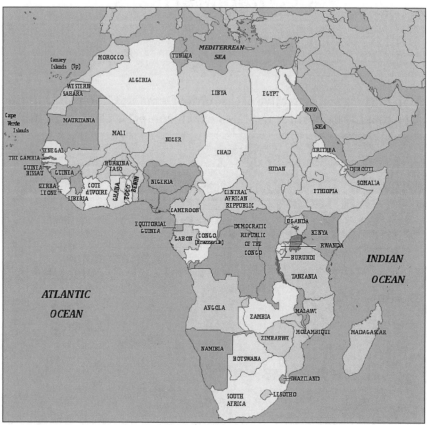

*Source: http://www.yourchildlearns.com/online-atlas/africa-map.htm*

12

## Map showing the countries in or bordering the Atlantic Ocean

*Source: http.www.map-monde*

# List of abbreviations

| | |
|---|---|
| ACP | African, Caribbean and Pacific States |
| AfDB | African Development Bank |
| AGOA | African Growth and Opportunity Act, adopted by the United States |
| AU | African Union |
| BASE | Basic Analysis and Security Engine |
| BEM | *Breveté d'Etat-Major* (qualified army General Staff) |
| CENCO | *la Conférence épiscopale nationale du Congo* (National episcopal conference of the Congo) |
| CICOS | *la Commission Internationale du Bassin Congo Oubangui Shari* (or International Commission for the Congo Basin Oubangui Shari) |
| CIDA | The Canadian International Development Agency |
| CNECI | *Caisse Nationale d'Épargne et de Crédit Immobilier* (or national savings and mortgage bank) |
| COHYDRO | *La Congolaise des Hydrocarbures*, (the DRC's national oil company) |
| COMESA | Common Market for Eastern and Southern Africa |
| CONAKAT | *Confédération Nationale du Katanga* (the Katanga National Federation) |
| CRENK | Centre for Research and Nuclear Studies in Kinshasa |
| CSDP | Common Security and Defence Policy |
| CSM | *Centre Supérieur Militaire de Kinshasa* (Higher Military Academy of Kinshasa) |
| CTA | *Conférence Tricontinental Atlantique* (or Tricontinental Atlantic Conference) |
| DRC | Democratic Republic of the Congo |
| DSCRP | *Document de la Stratégie de Croissance et de Réduction de la Pauvrété* (Document for growth strategy and poverty reduction) |
| ECCAS | Economic Community of Central African States |
| ECGLC | Economic Community of the Great Lakes Countries |

| | |
|---|---|
| ECOWAS | Economic Community of West African States |
| EFATBL | *École de Formation en Auto-Blindée* (Armoured Car Training School) |
| EFO | *École de Formation des Officiers de Kananga* (Kananga Officers' Training School) |
| EPA | Economic Partnership Agreement between the European Union and the six ACP regions |
| ERC | *École Royale des Cadets* (Royal School for Cadets) |
| ERM | *École Royale Militaire* (Royal Military School) |
| EU | European Union |
| EUFOR | European Union Military Force |
| EUPOL | European Union Police |
| EUSEC | European Union mission to advise and assist with reform of the security sector in the DRC |
| FAO | (UN) Food and Agriculture Organization |
| FAPLA | Armed Forces for the Liberation of Angola |
| FARDC | DRC Armed Forces |
| FLEGT | Forest Law Enforcement, Governance and Trade |
| G20 | Group of Twenty Finance Ministers and Central Bank Governors |
| GATT | General Agreement on Tariffs and Trade |
| GDP | Gross Domestic Product |
| GÉCAMINES | *Générale des Carrières et des Mines* |
| GHG | Greenhouse Gases |
| GMW | Guaranteed Minimum Wage |
| HIPC | Heavily Indebted Poor Countries |
| HIV/AIDS | Human immunodeficiency virus/acquired immunodeficiency syndrome |
| IAA | International African Association |
| ICRGL | International Conference on the Region of the Great Lakes |
| IIASA | International Institute for Applied Systems Analysis |
| IISS | International Institute of Strategic Studies in London |
| ILO | International Labour Organisation |
| IMF | International Monetary Fund |
| INERA | *Institut National pour les Etudes et la Recherche Agronomiques du Congo* (or the National Institute for Agronomic Study and Research in the Congo) |

| | |
|---|---|
| INSEE | *Institut National des Statistiques et des Études Économiques* (National Institute for Statistics and Economic Research) |
| ICAO | International Civil Aviation Organization |
| IPAD | Infrastructure Partnership for African Development |
| ISC | Independent State of the Congo |
| LDC | Least Developed Country |
| LTA | Lake Tanganyika Authority |
| MDA | DRC's Ministry for Agrarian Development |
| MDG | Millennium Development Goals |
| MDS | DRC's Ministry for Social Development |
| MEA | Multilateral Environmental Agreements |
| MIBA | *Minière de Bakwanga* (Bakwanga Mining Company) |
| MONUC | United Nations Organization Mission in the Democratic Republic of the Congo |
| NAFTA | North American Free Trade Agreement |
| NATO | North Atlantic Treaty Organisation |
| NBI | Nile Basin Initiative |
| NEPAD | New Partnership for African Development |
| NPT | Treaty on the Non-Proliferation of Nuclear Weapons |
| OAU | Organisation of African Unity |
| OCA | *Office des Cités Africaines* (DRC's office for African housing projects) |
| OGEDEP | *Office de Gestion de la Dette Publique* (Public debt management office of the DRC) |
| OKIMO | *Office des Mines d'Or de Kilo-Moto* (Kilo-Moto Gold Mines Office) |
| ONATRA | *Office National des Transports* (DRC's national transport office) |
| ONL | *Office National du Logement* (DRC's national housing office) |
| PAA | Brazilian programme for the acquisition of foodstuffs |
| PAM | *Programme Agricole Minimum* (DRC's minimum agricultural programme) |
| $PEG_1$ | *Premier Programme Économique du Gouvernement* (DRC Government's first Economic Programme) |
| $PEG_2$ | *Deuxième Programme Économique du Gouvernement* (second programme) |

| | |
|---|---|
| PESC | *Politique Étrangère et de Sécurité Commune* (DRC's foreign policy and mutual security) |
| PIR | *Programme Intérimaire Renforcé* (DRC's Provisional reinforced programme) |
| PMPTR | *Programme Minimum de Partenariat pour la Transition et la Relance* (DRC's Minimum partnership programme for transition and revival) |
| PMURR | *Programme Multisectoriel d'Urgence et Reconstruction et de Réhabilitation* (DRC's emergency, reconstruction and rehabilitation, multisector programme) |
| PNSAR | *Programme National de Relance du Secteur Agricole et Rural* (DRC's national programme for revival of the agricultural and rural sector) |
| PRAAL | *Programme d'Autosuffisance Alimentaire* (DRC's self-sufficiency in food programme) |
| PRGF | Poverty Reduction and Growth Facility |
| PRONAF | Brazilian body supporting family farms |
| REDD | Reducing Emission from Deforestation and Forest Degradation in Developing Countries (UN Programme) |
| RSA | Republic of South Africa |
| SADC | The Southern African Development Community |
| SDR | Special Drawing Rights |
| SIPRI | Stockholm International Peace Research Institute |
| SNEL | *Société Nationale d'Électricité* (National electric company) |
| SOMINKI | *Société Minière du Kivu* (Kivu Mining Company) |
| SOTEXKIN | *Société Textile de Kinshasa* (Kinshasa Textile Company |
| UN | United Nations |
| UNAZA | *Université Nationale du Zaïre* (National University of Zaire) |
| UNDP | UN Development Programme |
| UNESCO | UN Educational, Scientific and Cultural Organization |
| UNFPA | UN Population Fund |
| UNICEF | UN Children's Fund |
| UPI | Unity of Integrated Police (EU unit in the DRC) |
| USA | United States of America |
| US-AFRICOM | US Military Command for Africa |

| | |
|---|---|
| USSR | United Soviet Socialist Republics |
| UTEXAFRICA | *Usine Textile d'Afrique* (African Textile Factory |
| WB | World Bank |
| WESTCOR | Western Power Corridor Project |
| WHO | World Health Organization |
| WTO | World Trade Organization |
| ZIC | *Zones d'Intérêts Communs* (Mutual interest zones, with Angola) |

# General introduction

Never before have the issues raised by the future of DRC been accorded such urgency by the Congolese themselves, to the point of becoming a priority within a new development plan to be adopted. After the failure to expand the models based on Afro-European cooperation, the time has now come for a triangular structure covering the three continents of America, Europe and Africa, within the framework of a new and mutually beneficial partnership.

It may appear a little strange to mention the transatlantic policy of DRC, even though it is very true that this title bears the Europe-North America stamp, rooted in history and western culture. The arrangement mentioned does not exactly imply any contempt, since the well-trodden paths of a bygone era – that known as the Cold War – have been abandoned in order to take steps along a path that the 21$^{st}$ century is mapping out. The new vision is becoming clear.

Over a number of years, several attempts had been made, by both the public and private sectors, to consider transatlantic ties in the light of globalisation and changes worldwide, especially since the fall of the Berlin Wall in 1989[1].

There is no longer any question of relationships of power maintained exclusively between Europe and North America, but now firm relations aiming at a mutually advantageous cooperation, though not universal, do exist in general terms at least amongst the countries who share a common coastline with the Atlantic Ocean. Similar ties have been observed for some time now, especially between Brazil and Portugal, between one country in the Southern and the other in the Northern Hemisphere. This may also be observed in the ties between Angola and

---

[1]    In particular see KISSINGER, H., *La nouvelle puissance américaine*, Paris, Fayard, 2003, pp. 35-88; VERGNIOLLE DE CHANTAL, F., "Les débats américains sur la relation transatlantique", *Synthèse n° 128, Centre français sur les États-Unis*, Paris, March 2004.

Brazil, two States from the southern hemisphere. Why should we not also mention the privileged links that have existed for several centuries between Spain and its former colonies along the Atlantic coastline, such as Argentina and Mexico?

The three-continent Atlantic initiative, involving America, Europe and Africa comes at an appropriate time given the opportunities for cooperation between the three continents and in various fields.

## A. THE NEW PERCEPTION OF TRANSATLANTIC RELATIONS

Transatlantic relations are to-date still dominated by European-American alliances, strengthened during the Cold War by the creation of the North Atlantic Treaty Organisation (NATO), which aimed to counteract the Soviet threat in Europe and worldwide.

The breaking up of the USSR and its empire, the collapse of Communism, as a homogenous political bloc, the fall of the Berlin Wall, the establishment of democracies in eastern Europe and various regions in the world, notably in Africa, the liberalisation of commercial trade, the concerted fight against terrorism, drug trafficking and international criminal activity, the protection and preservation of the environment especially to combat global warming, the respect of human rights and basic freedoms are so many factors to influence a realignment of transatlantic relations.

The ending of the Cold War and hence East-West bipolarity enabled NATO to expand to the Eastern European countries, and former members of the Warsaw Pact (Bulgaria, Hungary, Poland, etc.). This new order involves changes to strategic considerations, particularly the identification of current and future threats, but also in dealings with Russia, a nuclear power and permanent member of the Security Council.

Even though the values and strategic interests between North America and Europe remain convergent (the endorsement of the State of law, democratic principles and human rights, the promotion of a market economy, the fight against terrorism and international criminality, the non-proliferation of nuclear weapons, etc.), nevertheless we are witnessing a diversification, on the part of the United States of America, of partnerships based on vested interests and their geographical situation[2]. Canada's interest in Africa in particular keeps on increasing.

Is there also a place for Africa in renewed transatlantic relationships, for both American-African and also European-African ties? DRC, a country located at the heart of the African Continent and endowed with so much potential, ought to play an active part in the rebirth of a three-continent Atlantic alliance.

Several areas for cooperation have already been identified, notably[3]:

"(i)    The management of the Atlantic Ocean: an area for reciprocal trade and communications;

(ii)    Energy: a zone for off-shore oil exploration and exploitation; cooperation on renewable energy sources;

(iii)   Agriculture: Latin America and Africa are considered as two important but very little exploited "agricultural frontiers". The Atlantic area may appreciably influence international trade in agricultural produce and contribute to the eradication of hunger in the world.

(iv)    The elimination of the extreme poverty and hunger which is the primary objective of the Millenium Development Goals adopted by heads of State and governments in 2000 at the initiative of the United Nations;

(v)     Water: access to drinking water remains an imperative for development for several countries in the Southern Hemisphere;

(vi)    The struggle against global warming and the defence of biodiversity: the Atlantic area possesses the two largest Equatorial forests (Brazil and Centrl Africa). They account for much of the absorption of greenhouse gases;

(vii)   The countries along the Atlantic coastline ought to actively participate in the international protection of the Arctic and the Antarctic. The two poles play an significant role in regulating the world's climate;

(viii)  Migratory movement of populations and development: the Atlantic area ought to encourage people's free movement in order

---

[2]    Cf. VERGNIOLLE DE CHANTAL, F., *op. cit.*, p. 2.
[3]    See *Agenda du Futur*, Forum "Pour une initiative tricontinentale atlantique", http://www.itca.hcp.ma.

to keep up their intermingling tradition. A transatlantic cooperation in this domain would take account of the links between
immigration and development;

(ix)   Education: especially in the sectors at the cutting edge, putting a
       particular emphasis on scientific research and the training of the
       labour force;
(x)    New technologies;
(xi)   Peace and security;
(xii)  The consolidation of the State of law and democracy."

## B.  THE ECONOMIC AND STRATEGIC ISSUES

The importance of the Atlantic at the economic and strategic levels
is not in doubt. It divides Europe and Africa from the Americas, and
covers 106,200,000 km$^2$. The glacial Arctic Ocean lies at its northern
boundary and a large part of the Antarctic Ocean at its southern
boundary, between the meridians of Cape Horn and the Cape Agulhas[4].
The Antarctic is part of mankind's common heritage. The Antarctic
Treaty on 1 December 1959 sets out the conditions for its exploitation[5].

The Atlantic area represents two-thirds of the world's GNP and
almost 70% of global consumption. The Atlantic is a favoured route
for countries around it and acts as a conduit for a large proportion of
worldwide sea and air traffic[6]. Several deep-water sea ports have been
created: Montreal, New York, Antwerp, Rotterdam, Le Havre, Casa-
blanca, Lagos, Douala, Lomé, Pointe-Noire, Abidjan, for example.

More than half of the planet's renewable freshwater sources and
substantial reserves of hydrocarbons and minerals, but also forests and
arable land (the globe's great agricultural frontiers) are concentrated
around the Atlantic area.

---

[4]   Cf. *Dictionnaire encylopédique Alpha*, vol. 2, Lausanne, Grammont, 1983,
pp. 220-221.
[5]   Text of the Treaty published: DUPUY, P.-M., p. 777. The first article proclaims:
"Antarctica shall be used for peaceful purposes only. There shall be prohibited, *inter
alia*, any measures of a military nature, such as the establishment of military bases
and fortifications, the carrying out of military maneuvers, as well as the testing of any
type of weapons."
[6]   Cf. *Agenda du Futur, op. cit.*

Kofi ANNAN was right when he emphasised that the Atlantic countries are privileged and offer vast opportunities for transnational cooperation. Hence the "Tricontinental Atlantic" initiative is indicative of the increasing and endless opportunities in prospect[7].

Since the end of the Second World War and based upon Article 52 of the United Nations' Charter, the Northern Hemisphere countries have set up a mechanism for collective security through NATO, supported by national systems for defence and security.

Because of the nuclear deterrent and arms control, the North Atlantic area is a peaceful zone. However, this region still has to counter new threats from: terrorism, drug trafficking and transnational criminal activities, for example. The tricontinental collaboration is in place to overcome these scourges and make the transatlantic area more secure. Remarkable progress has been achieved by the Southern Hemisphere countries to create peaceful non-nuclear zones, although there have been some attempts against the democratic process. The mechanisms for collective security within several regional and economic organisations are worthy of support. This is the case for the Economic Community of West African States (ECOWAS), Economic Community of Central African States (ECCAS) and the South African Development Community (SADC)[8].

On 6 February 2007, in order to work alongside African countries on matters of peace and security, the United States of America created the military US Africa Command (US AFRICOM) as the sixth united geographical command within the unified commands of the Defense Department[9].

US AFRICOM has the following main objectives[10]:

– to demonstrate the strategic importance of Africa, for peace and stability on the continent for Africans, the United States and the rest of the international community;

---

[7]   Declaration made at the abovementioned Forum "for a tricontinental Atlantic initiative".
[8]   See the constitutional texts in: TSHIBANGU, K., *Code des Organisationales*, Brussels, Bruylant, 2008.
[9]   See US AFRICOM, http://www.africom.mil/index.fr.asp.
[10]   *Ibid.*

– to enable the United States to improve the management of its resources to better support American initiatives to help African countries, the African Union and the regional economic communities;
– To give the African countries and regional organisations an integrated centre to collaborate with the Department of Defense better to communicate their security requirements;
– To help the African people to marginalise the enemies of peace, to prevent conflicts, to strengthen legitimate institutions and stable and just governments, but also to support the development of civil society; etc.

For several years the European Union has been attempting to establish the common foreign and security policy (CFSP), as mentioned in the European Union's Treaty of Maastricht on 7 February 7 1992[11].

In the framework of the CFSP the European Union Council authorised the military offensive and deployment, from 12 June to 1 September 2003, of an operation called "Artemis" under French command, to stabilise and make the Ituri District in the Eastern Province of DRC safe in order to guarantee the election process in this part of the country[12].

The Council organised a second military mission in DRC called "EUFOR" to ensure security for the elections organised in 2006, as support for the United Nations Organization Mission in the Democratic Republic of Congo (MONUC)[13].

The Atlantic Southern Hemisphere area is taking part in efforts by the international community to at least limit, if not prohibit, nuclear arms' proliferation, by concluding two regional treaties: the Treaty of Tlatelolco of 14 February 1967 aimed at prohibiting nuclear weapons in

---

[11] Treaty text in: Union européenne, *Recueil des traités*, Volume I, Brussels, Luxemburg, 1993, p. 11.
[12] Cf. MAVUNGU, J.-P., *"Le rôle de l'Union européenne dans le processus de démocratisation en RDC"*, in *Participation et responsabilité des acteurs dans un contexte d'émergence démocratique en Républque du Congo*, Articles from the scientific days at the Law Faculty of the University of Kinshasa, 18-19 June 2007, Kinshasa, Presses de l'Université de Kinshasa, 2007, p. 231.
[13] *Ibid.*

Latin America and the Caribbean, as well as the Treaty of Pelindaba of 11 April 1996 on a nuclear weapon free zone in Africa[14].

Both regions have a valid role to play in the international debate on the non-proliferation of nuclear weapons[15].

## C. THE PRINCIPLES OF THE DRC'S FOREIGN POLICY[16]

DRC is one of the countries bordering the Atlantic Ocean, via the Bas-Congo province. Forty kilometres long, this coastal area is the only opening to the world by sea. The economic advantages are clear: means of commercial trade, the wealth of fish, oil and tourist potential, rights to fly over the air space over internal water and territorial sea areas...

As party to the Montego Bay Agreement of 10 December, 1982 on the law of the sea, DRC has adopted a law on its territorial waters[17]. This is aimed at a better protection of its interests at sea, especially on the continental shelf. The defence of national interests as well as both regional and international cooperation are not antonymic.

As a member of the United Nations Organisation (UN) since 20 September 1960 which is less than three months after its accession to international sovereignty, DRC had to take into account the principles enshrined in the Charter and in the definition of its foreign policy[18].

---

[14]  Cf. United Nations, *Statement of multilateral agreements on disarmament and the control of arms*, New York, 1998.

[15]  For an analysis of this matter, see in particular, United Nations, "*The United Nations and nuclear non-proliferation*", New York, 1995.

[16]  On foreign policy see in particular CHARILLON, F., *Politique étrangère. Nouveau regards*, Paris, Presses de Sciences Po, 2002; GRAWITZ, M. and LECA, J., *Traité de science politique. Les Politiques publiques*, vol. 4, Paris, Presses Universitaires de France, 1985; LBANA, L. et LOFEMBE, B., *La politique étrangère de la République Démocratique du Congo. Structures, fonctionnement et manifestations*, Kinshasa, Sirius, 2008; MWAYILA, T., *La politique étrangère de la République Démocratique du Congo. Continuités et ruptures*, Paris, l'Harmattan, 2009; NYEME, T., *Une diplomatie repensée pour la République Démocratique du Congo. Urgence et pertinence*, Kananga, Éd. Universitaires du Kasayai, 2001.

[17]  See Law n° 09/0002 of 7 May 2009 defining the limits of the DRC's territorial waters.

[18]  Cf. Article 2 of the United Nations Charter of 26 June 1945.

As a member since 1963 of the Organisation of African Unity (OAU), later to become the African Union [19], the internal factors (geography, economics, political regime, history, military information, etc) and external factors (part of Central Africa, international environment, etc.) are features which have also been taken into account in the determination of the guiding principles of the DRC's foreign policy.

Amongst the latter, there should be included: good neighbour relations, the African vocation, communication with the outside world, mutually advantageous regional and international cooperation, the peaceful settlement of disputes, no recourse to force, respect of the boundaries inherited from colonial period [20], etc.

## 1. Good neighbour relations

The shared borders with nine countries require DRC to adopt a policy of good neighbour relations, based on the desire for peace and cooperation by respecting their respective sovereignties.

The policy of good neighbour relations is dictated by geography, apart from its legal basis [21]. A vast country with several others at its borders raises serious problems for defence. Tensions or the risks of tensions at the borders are almost permanent.

DRC maintains diplomatic relations with its nine neighbours in application of this principle. Relations with Burundi, Uganda and Rwanda have just returned to normality, notably by exchanging ambassadors, after several years' estrangement following the war of aggression that these three countries mounted against DRC on 2 August 1998, even though it is true that much still remains to be done.

---

[19] For the text of the Charter of the OAU, of 25 May 1963 and the constitutional Act of the African Union, see TSHIBANGU, K., *op. cit.*, pp. 1243 and 1911.

[20] These principles were reaffirmed by the Head of State during the opening of the 10th diplomatic conference held in Kinshasa, from 2 to 7 December 2002, and during the investiture speech given on 6 December 2006. See the Ministry for Foreign Affairs and International Cooperation, *Actes de la 10e Conférence diplomatique*, Kinshasa, 2003, p. 83.

[21] The preamble to the United Nations Charter proclaims: "We the peoples of the United Nations determined ... to practice tolerance and live together in peace and with one another as good neighbours (...)". Article 1, paragraph 2, affirms that States must develop friendly relations.

Learning from the past, problems in abeyance with neighbouring countries need to be addressed and lasting solutions proposed. Regular meetings with Congolese leaders and those from neighbouring countries, including those between heads of State and government, will be likely to prevent some crises and to facilitate the peaceful settlement of disputes that arise.

Relations with Atlantic neighbours open up new perspectives and should enable DRC to play a full role in the context of tricontinental discussions.

## 2. The African vocation

The promotion of African cooperation is the logical complement to the good neighbour relations policy. By virtue of the DRC's central position, unity in the continent can only originate from here. Was it not Franz FANON who said "Africa has the shape of a revolver whose trigger lies in Congo"?[22]

The DRC's African vocation is due as much to its geography as to its history.

The geostrategic position that it holds in the centre of the African continent, its potential and demographics make it one of the unifying forces in Africa, just like South Africa and Nigeria.

For several decades, DRC has been involved in African causes, especially regional integration and the struggle against colonialism and apartheid.

The policy for regional groupings enables DRC to take part in the creation of several regional and sub-regional organisations (the Organisation of African Unity later known as the African Union, the African Development Bank, the Economic Community of the Great Lake Countries, the Economic Community of Central African States, etc.) and to be members of existing organisations (The Southern African Development Community and the Common Market for Eastern and Southern Africa).

The country's varied membership of regional and sub-regional organisations is far from being a handicap; it involves improved coordin-

---

[22]  FANON, F., *Pour la Révolution africaine*, Paris, La Découverte, 1964.

ation to better identify the country's interests and the objectives to be achieved, but is also an appropriate mobilisation for human, financial and logistical resources.

Nowadays the DRC's African vocation can be attributed to three pillars: regional integration, African solidarity and regular discussions with regional powers and friendly countries.

Regional integration[23], which began in the 1960s with the creation of the OAU in 1963, is worthy of consideration and consolidation as a means for reconciliation between peoples, promoting unity and peace amongst States.

In time, regional integration will permit the migration from micro-nationalism to macro-nationalism through the free circulation of goods and people, the establishment of integration projects[24], intensification of commercial trade, harmonisation in business law[25], consolidation of economic and monetary cooperation, and the complementary nature of industrial, agricultural and social policies, etc.

African solidarity could be demonstrated by the strengthening of South-South cooperation, development aid, assistance to persons suffering after natural catastrophes, sheltering people after conflicts, participation in peace missions within the UN and the African Union, etc.

Regular discussions with regional authorities and friendly countries are required to adopt a common position on several international issues: the regulation of international trade, environmental protection, management of migrating persons, reform of international institutions, fight against disease (HIV/AIDS, malaria, tuberculosis, etc.) protection of works of art, the determination of regulatory reserves and raw material prices, etc.

---

[23]  For an analysis of this issue, see in particularly DIUOF, M., *L'intégration économ-ique. Perspectives africaines,* Dakar, Nouvelles Éditions africaines, 1983; NDESHYO RURIHOSE, *Le système d'intégration africaine,* Kinshasa, Presses universitaires du Zaïre, 1984.

[24]  See the New Partnership for Africa's Development (NEPAD) October 2001.

[25]  See the Treaty of 17 October on the "Organisation for the Harmonisation of Business Law in Africa" (OHADA). The Treaty text published by TSHIBANGU, K., *op. cit.* p. 1557. The RDC joined OHADA in February 2010.

## 3. Communication with the outside world

As a member of the international community, DRC has been applying the policy of communicating with the outside world ever since it achieved independence, as no country can afford the luxury of living in isolation.

The peoples of the Central African kingdoms and empires were in contact with the outside world well before the instigation of colonialism, principally because of evangelist missionaries, trade and the slave trade. The Kongo kingdom, for example, had dealings with Portugal, Spain and the Holy See as long ago as the 15th century[26].

Articles 1 and 13a of the General Act of the Berlin Conference on 26 February 1885 included freedom of trade and free access to the sea for all nations.

The policy of openness, called the "open door" policy, consists in maintaining relations with all countries, without exception, and keeping some balance between partners. This policy was demonstrated by establishing diplomatic relations with several countries around the world and participating in different international institutions, such as the UN and its specialist and allied bodies (World Bank, IMF, ILO, UNESCO, WHO, ICAO, FAO, etc.).

Additionally, DRC has diplomatic relations with several countries, including the Atlantic countries.

## 4. Mutually advantageous regional and international cooperation

As a developing country, DRC benefits from regional and international cooperation. Regional cooperation is principally in the form of membership of organisations on the continent (AU, AfDB, BASE, etc.) and sub-regional organisations (ECCAS, ECGLC, SADC, COMESA). Due to the establishment of new institutions resulting from the general and democratic elections of 2006, DRC is gradually finding its place in the regional and international arena. In fact, it has hosted two sub-regional summits: the 29th SADC summit of heads of State and govern-

---

[26] See CORNEVIN, R., *Histoire du Zaïre. Des origines à nos jours*, Brussels/Paris, Hayez-Académie des Sciences d'Outre-Mer, 1989; NDAYWEL è EZIEM, I, *Nouvelle histoire du Congo. Des origines à la République démocratique*, Brussels/Kinshasa, CRI-Afrique Éditions, 2009.

ment, in September 2009, and also the 14th ECCAS summit of heads of State and government, in October 2009.

The SADC summit in September 2009 placed a particular emphasis on trade, energy, the impact of the economic and financial crises on economies as well as on the Millenium Development Goals (MDG), food security and development issues[27]. The Kinshasa-Luanda-Pretoria axis could give impetus to cooperation within the SADC.

The ECCAS summit in October 2009 dealt with several matters likely to strengthen cooperation between member States: peace, stability and security, trade, the free circulation of people and goods, economic and monetary union, environment and the management of natural resources, the drafting of a common agricultural policy, etc.[28]

DRC shares land area and resources with neighbouring ECCAS Atlantic countries: the tropical forests, Congo Basin, oil reserves in the Gulf of Guinea, fish stocks, the animals, etc.

The management, exploitation and preservation of these land areas and resources need rigorous cooperation.

As a post-conflict country, DRC has been bestowed with a Document for the Strategy for Growth and Reduction of Poverty (DSCRP)[29]. This contains five guiding principles to be followed with support from bi- and multi-lateral partners within the framework of international cooperation. They are:

- to uphold good governance and consolidate peace by the strengthening of institutions;
- to build up macroeconomic stability and growth;
- to improve access to social services and reduce vulnerability;
- to fight HIV/AIDS;
- to support community dynamics.

The implementation of development diplomacy should enable DRC to muster external support (financial resources, technology transfers, the strengthening of capacity, and a variety of aid) in order to reduce

---

[27]   Cf. *Le Potential* n° 4721 of 9 September 2009, p. 3.
[28]   Cf. *Le Palmarès* n° 4666 of 26 October 2009, p. 3.
[29]   Cf. DRC, *Document de la startégie de croissance et de réduction de la pauvreté* (DSCRP), Kinshasa, July 2006.

poverty by the achievement of the Millenium Development Goals (MDG) and the DSCRP.

The application of the policy of openness to the outside world has enabled DRC to maintain multi-sector relations for cooperation with both bi- and multi-lateral partners.

The principal partners around the Atlantic are recruited in the North (Germany, Belgium, Canada, United States, France, United Kingdom, etc.) and in the South (South Africa, Angola, Brazil, Morocco, Nigeria, Namibia, Congo Brazzaville, Gabon, etc.). Various bodies of the United Nations Organisation, the World Bank, the IMF and the European Union are the main multilateral partners.

Certainly, the diversification of partners and the funds allocated were beneficial and enabled projects in various fields to be carried out (health, agriculture, education, infrastructure, etc.). However, international cooperation has not fundamentally changed the situation in the country. The rate of development is not outstanding[30].

The breakdown of the cooperation established with various partners from the North and some international institutions in the 1990s owing to the lack of democracy and violations of human rights has had a harmful effect on national living standards. The conflicts that cast a dark shadow over the country from 1996 to-date were not going to facilitate any sustainable development for the Congolese people and strengthen international cooperation. The system for public assistance for development has been changed in favour of humanitarian assistance and emergency aid to the detriment of investment projects.

Straight after the war and in the current phase of the country's reconstruction, fresh cooperation guidelines have been adopted by DRC in order to revitalise relations with its partners:

–   cooperation agreements based on reciprocal advantages should maintain the State's sovereignty and be conducive to economic independence;
–   competition between external partners will have to be considered as ancillary and isolated matters, external aid should be to finance the

---

[30]   Cf. DRC, DSCRP, *op. cit.*

difference in cost between development requirements and national resources;

– development projects negotiated with external partners will have to be compatible with the priorities established in the public investment programme[31].

At the same time, DRC which has its own place in Africa and on the world stage, has to stand up and free itself of current huge burdens such as wars, insurgency, lack of authority, corruption, nepotism and violations of human rights to become competitive and show its mettle in transatlantic relations.

This fresh approach, which shakes up the old order, devalues the transatlantic Western Europe-North America alliance, and clearly demonstrates the benefits that the countries surrounding the Southern Atlantic are able to offer, as a vehicle to stimulate the world towards a greater affinity, even if threatened by the volume of trade across the Pacific and Indian Oceans.

With this perspective, DRC should play an active role in this new vision of transatlantic relations, likely to group all the countries around the Atlantic coastline in one recognisable organisation, with due account given to the various relationships and many forms of cooperation.

---

[31] Ministry of Foreign Affairs and International Cooperation, *Acts...*, *op. cit.*, p. 30.

# Plan of this work

The book is structured in three parts.

The first section entitled "DRC, undeniable assets compared to those of Brazil", shows the geostrategic importance of the DRC amongst the major transatlantic countries based on historical and geopolitical data. It also explains the cultural and sociological issues which clearly put the position of Congolese society in the picture of transatlantic relations.

The second part, entitled "DRC: economic potential in contrast with the level of development and realistic expectations", deals with the economic and social dimensions of the current crisis, as well as the diplomatic and social aspects aiming to stabilise the situation.

The third part entitled "The reasons to expect a prosperous and powerful future Congo" is a profession of faith. It describes the ways and means to make the Congo a sign of hope for its population and an opportunity for Africa and humankind. This is a profession of faith based on what the major sectors of development can bring – agriculture, nature conservation, water, energy and mining resources – on condition that these sectors are well managed and safe from economic and financial predators and corrupt officials, through the establishment of a State with a veritable legal system.

# PART ONE

# DRC, UNDENIABLE ASSETS COMPARED TO THOSE OF BRAZIL

# Introduction

It is interesting to show that DRC possesses, in spite of its current difficulties because of previously mentioned and serious preoccupations, major assets equally diverse as its natural and mining resources as well as the large size of its population and its youth, which still attract potential markets and numerous investors. These assets would be enough to justify its importance, as it does in a country such as Brazil which is strikingly similar to DRC.

However, for about five years, it has been noticeable that the country is stirring and intends to regain the position once held in international relations up to the first decade of independence at the end of the 1960s. A glorious past to be revived.

To appreciate this role, first the geography then geopolitics (Chapter I), the geostrategic factor (Chapter II) and then finally historical, cultural and sociological facts (Chapter III) are explained.

CHAPTER I

# From geography to geopolitics

It cannot be denied that geographical features help to give a special character to DRC. Its massive size determines the special ties between it and the countries at its borders.

In fact, the country extends from the Atlantic Ocean to the Eastern Plateau and makes up a large part of the Congo River Basin. In the North lies one of the largest areas of tropical forest in the world. The East borders the East African Great Rift, an area of mountains, hills, the Great Lakes, and also volcanoes. The South and centre, with areas of grassland and trees, form a high plateau rich in mineral ores. A coastline with the Atlantic Ocean, some forty kilometres long, lies in the West and north of the mouth of the River Congo.

## I. The geography

DRC (ex-Zaïre) is one of the Central African States. With its 2,345,409 km$^2$, it is the interface between several countries and is at the confluence of French- English-, Portuguese- and Arab-speaking countries. Situated between 5°2' latitude North and 13°5' latitude South, the country stretches from 12°51' to 31°15' longitude East. It has an undeniable geostrategic position at the heart of the African Continent: with an immense surface area (>2,345,000 km$^2$), with nine neighbouring counties along a 9,165 km border. The country shares borders with Angola and the Republic of Congo-Brazzaville to the West, the Central African Republic and Sudan to the North, Uganda, Rwanda, Burundi and Tanzania to the East, and Zambia and Angola to the South. An enviable position, when one considers that in international law, proximity confers a special quality to relationships between those States concerned.

The DRC is in a unique geostrategic position, especially because of its 68 million inhabitants. Thus there is a geological "excess" with the various deposits of minerals underground (copper, cobalt, coltan, zinc, gold, diamonds, oil, gas, methane, uranium, nickel, iron ore, manganese, niobium, germanium, cadmium, etc.). There is also an energy "excess" with its hydroelectric potential estimated at 100,000 MW, or 13 % of the world's hydroelectric capacity; the Inga site has been described as the integrating project in the framework of the regional and sub-regional cooperation (NEPAD, SADC and ECCAS). Moreover DRC possesses 47 % of the Central African tropical forest (with the entire Congo Basin covering 3.8 million km²).

At world level, DRC is the second country, after Brazil, to possess an important tropical rain forest, with more than 400 species of mammals and reptiles some of which risk becoming extinct.

Moreover, it also has a wide variety of plant species and large expanses of fertile land, ranked as the second country in the world in terms of the area of arable land available[32].

Its climate and vegetation are responsible for four equatorial climate zones in the basin with high temperatures, very heavy rainfall and dense forests (with temperatures between 23° and 30°C); two tropical climate zones favourable to savannah with scattered trees in the fourth North and South parallels (between 22° and 26.5°C); a zone with a high altitude climate, not so hot nor so well watered towards the East and South-East (between 16° and 22°C). To the South-East, the savannah is interspersed by numerous corridors of trees which bear witness to the volume of the water system, whilst vegetation covers the mountains in layers to the East, from the tropical forest to the high altitude prairies.

The natural frontiers (ocean, lakes, rivers, mountain peaks, etc.) provide the Congolese polygon with this topography. The Congolese have managed to establish their own space because successive generations have lived in this particular physical environment, defined by "*léopoldisme*" in the 19th century (because of the name, the Independent State of the Congo).

Territorial integrity has been secured over time, although it has been tested more than once by aborted attempts at separatism with support from outside the country. Few other African people have had to prove their rock-solid integrity, with their historic territoriality under attack in the aftermath of independence.

---

[32]   Cf. MAVUNGU, J.-P., "La République démocratique du Congo en quête d'un leadership régional", unpublished text.

DRC had to learn its lessons from the successive upheavals suffered.

The experience of geopolitics is that with support from transatlantic partners, some influence has already been brought to bear on African States.

## II. Geopolitics

In this area, DRC should also use its multifaceted influence (cultural, economic, military, etc.) in order to ensure both its survival and stability, especially at the borders where its security has been or is still under threat. The national sanctuary should be made unassailable, not only because of the development of modern technology, but also and above all due to the training of its leaders, especially in the fields of defence and security. In effect, the obstacles hindering the potential progress in the Congolese geopolitical situation arise more from the political volition of its leaders than from objective considerations. These handicaps will be overcome as long as the Congolese people established over a vast territory, second in area in Africa after Sudan was divided, and number one in natural resources, can be endowed with leaders capable of driving it towards a better future.

In the medium-term, a policy of dissuasion must be adopted and applied. More concretely, DRC should give itself the means and the strength to dissuade any State on its borders which would, either through political will or military power directly or indirectly start, including the use of mercenaries, a new war designed to erode its sovereignty or integrity. Hence DRC's territory and also its people would be made secure. To this end, the current organisation of National Defence needs to be revised in the context of the State's revival.

It is desirable to make use of the increased frequency of the two-yearly committee meetings between DRC and South Africa to promote friendly transatlantic ties. These committee meetings could help eradicate or nip in the bud any fresh military attacks or a follow-up to previous armed conflicts, being organised by those who still have a hostile intent towards DRC. Does the fact that the South African Republic has taken such an initiative not mean that DRC is an important Central African State in geopolitical terms? Does the tour by Secretary of State Hillary Clinton to a half-dozen African States, particularly to DRC, prior to the arrival of the American President Barack Obama, not also reinforce a similar conclusion ?

Finally, the message given by President Barack Obama, during his stop in Accra in March 2009, challenged the African continent to accept independence and responsibilities, and is already an invitation to foster new relationships between the West and Africa. DRC should kick-start its transatlantic policy, given its geostrategic position. Thus, there is a choice to be made of the utmost importance, as will be shown in the following pages.

CHAPTER II

# The geostrategic factor

Quite rare are those States which nature has given a geostrategic[33] position as favourable as that of DRC, as mentioned in the previous chapter. In this connection, no other African State can objectively be a rival to it; not the Republic of South Africa (RSA), off-centre from the continental and world axes, nor Nigeria, enclosed in the Gulf of Guinea. As we have also just noted, in Sub-Saharan Africa, DRC possesses immense and various mineral, energy, aquatic, forest and animal resources. Finally, it has great expanses of fertile and arable land, together with abundant rainfall. This very favourable geostrategic position and the variety and extent of resources make this country a potential economic power in Africa.

On the other side of the Atlantic, the geostrategic position of Brazil quite closely resembles that of Congo. For the first time since the end of the colonial era in Latin America in the 19th century, a political, diplomatic, economic, military, technological and scientific power has emerged, whose strength projects well beyond its borders, as far as Central Africa, including DRC.

## I. Brazil takes off

Officially independent since 7 September 1822 (but recognised as a sovereign State only since 29 August 1825), the Federal Republic of Brazil is the most extensive and highly populated country in Latin America, with a surface area of 8,514,877 km$^2$ (15 times that of France four times that of DRC) and a population of 190 million inhabitants. Portuguese is the official language; the real is its currency and its parity is currently 1 USD equivalent to 1.75 R$ (BRL)[34].

---

[33] According to EMERSON, B., *Léopold II – Le royaume est l'empire*, Paris, Gembloux, Duculot, 1980, the northern border alone of the Congo acquires a strategic importance as a means of access to the Nile.
[34] www.wikipedia.org, the geography and history of Brazil.

Brazil also managed to turn the wheel of history in its favour like the United States of America had done before. This proves that a well-organised developing country can develop and even surpass its former colonial power, one of the great world powers since the 15ᵗʰ century. As soon as the Brazilian Government dominated its inland and maritime territory, its air space and outer space with the launch into space of a rocket, Brazil may be included in the ranks of the Great Countries. As the first major country in South America to show interest in DRC, Brazil may become a strategic partner. Hence there is an opportunity for Congo to take off, after Brazil or India, since the country has, without any bias, all the assets required.

In 2007, President Lula of Brazil officially expressed his intention to come and share the experience of his country with Congolese people by means of a communication given to both houses of Parliament united for a special session[35].

An official Brazilian document "reaffirms that the territorial distance between different regions is not capable of destroying world-wide visions (...) nor the cultural bases which are a part of shared history"[36]. According to this document, "an important contingent of Africans, reduced to slavery, came in the main from the region known today as the Democratic Republic of Congo and has had a profound and marked influence on the way of thinking, customs, religion and national superstitions"[37]. Also included therein: "since 2003, the government of President Luiz Ignacio Lula da Sylva, in recognition of the contribution from the peoples of Africa to the creation of the Brazilian identity, has become close to Africa, and instigated law 10639 making it compulsory to teach Afro-Brazilian history and culture in the school programme"[38].

---

[35] Letter from President Luiz Inacio DA SILVA to the Presidents of both houses of the Congolese Parliament, March 2007.
[36] *Brasil Congo, Olhares Cruzados, Diadema, Kinshasa,* Sao Paulo, Reflexo Editora, 2007, p. 9.
[37] *Ibid.,* p. 9.
[38] *Ibid.*

## A. HOW HAS BRAZIL MANAGED ITS DEVELOPMENT?

The results of the extraordinary growth and the awakening of Brazil are currently visible with the expansion of exports, discovery of hydro-carbons, financial stability, inflation mastered, increased internal and external investments, a greater consumer demand, social programmes aimed at the needy and democratic political cohesion.

More than one reason would persuade DRC to maintain all-out cooperation with the Federal Republic of Brazil which, on the world stage today, occupies a strategically important place due to its flourishing economy, showing it to be an unrivalled model of a modern country in the third world and an emerging power from the Southern Hemisphere.

The Brazilian government understood soon enough that nothing could be expected from an impoverished population traumatised by all sorts of social injustice. Its first priority was the determined fight against hunger and social misery. This was the famous programme "zero hunger" launched in 2003 and whose aims were to guarantee the fundamental right of every Brazilian to food, to promote food and nutritional security, and to eradicate extreme poverty.

To achieve its aim, the government set in place a ministry for social development and the struggle to combat hunger (MDS) and which coordinates a vast and integrated network for protection and social promotion based around four complementary axes:

1) alimentary and nutritional security;
2) social assistance;
3) the conditional transfer of revenue to the poor;
4) the creation of opportunities for the poor.

The priority given by the government to the formation of a national network for social protection and promotion is reflected in the evolution of the budget of the Ministry for social development and the struggle to combat hunger. This budget, amounting to 4 billion US dollars in 2003, doubled in five years (to 8 billion US dollars in 2008).

The diversification of the Brazilian economy is now founded on solid sectors such as agriculture, mining, industry, energy (biocar-burants and oil) and on infrastructure, sectors which have all bene-fited from a combination of new technologies and hefty incentives for private investment, to a point where the GNP (gross national product) amounts to 1580 billion dollars, which puts Brazil among the first ten world economies.

The Brazilian plan to tie economic development to social development casts real doubts upon the traditional and very "economist" approach, which maintains that economic growth automatically involves social cohesion. This is innovative because this plan supports the opposite view; social cohesion is and must be considered as an element of growth.

Today, the figures speak for themselves in terms of the results and clearly show that the Brazilian economy experienced a 5.4% growth in 2007. This growth is in line with social development; 6.9 million jobs were created between 2003 and 2008. The minimum salary has had a real increase of 53% since 2003.

A significant part of this growth is attributable to social policies which redistribute revenue and widens the internal market by incorporating the poorest as consumers of goods.

This Brazilian development concept which has proved so successful drew its inspiration from ideas of José De Castro (1908-1973) for whom disregarding the problem of hunger in the political and intellectual agenda of the country during the colonial and post-colonial periods can be likened to a conspiracy of silence. It attaches great importance to agriculture which gives work to the people as well as nourishing them.

## 1. Agriculture [39]

Considered as one of the breadbaskets of the world, Brazil owes its expansion to agrarian reform mainly based on intensive and highly mechanised agriculture. It is the world's top producer of coffee, soybean, sugar, wood, maize and cocoa. It is also second in the world for the production of cotton, beans, tobacco and cassava.

Simultaneous with the intensification and mechanisation of agriculture, the Brazilian government initiated policies to encourage small-scale farmers to make each district of this vast national territory self-sufficient in food, to enable every family in rural areas to overcome the

---

[39] Alternatives Sud, *Retour de l'État: pour quelles politiques sociales? Points de vue du Sud*, Centre tricontinental, Syllepse, Volume XVI-2009, Paris, pp. 171-182.

scourge of hunger and then to generate a surplus of revenue to confront other basic needs such as health care, schooling, housing, clothing, etc.

Its policy in this area is based upon support to family farms (PRONAF) and the programme for acquiring foodstuffs (PAA). The PRONAF, established by the Ministry for Agrarian Development (MDA) in association with the Ministry for Social Development (MDS) operates a wide-ranging micro-credit and rural technical assistance system for small-scale producers throughout the country. For the 2007-2008 campaign, 5.1 billion euros were made available for this programme.

The PAA, under the authority of the MDS, plays a role complementary to that of the PRONAF in the promotion of food and nutritional security, to both the producer and the consumer. Through the operation of this programme, the government guarantees the purchase of food produced by family farms exempt from tender bids, at prices in line with those operated on the markets by the large distribution centres.

Brazil has the leading world position for producing cattle due, in particular, to the advanced method of artificial insemination, not forgetting, pig and poultry production which make it one of the great leaders in livestock production.

After the fall in the world economy, otherwise known as the financial crisis, during 2008 and which had a major effect on the world food crisis, excellent results have been recorded in Brazil for agrarian and livestock production (wood, wood, coffee, sugar, soybean, milk, meat, etc.) thanks to the 107.5 billion BRL budget allocation provided by the Brazilian federal government in June 2009.

The profit obtained in this sector enabled the range of agricultural machinery to be improved and modernised and the impact is demonstrated by the creation of 52,927 jobs.

## 2. Mining resources

Brazil, just like DRC, is known for its vast mining resources. It has substantial reserves of iron, manganese, copper, tin, niobium, bauxite, zinc, gold, nickel, lead, potassium, titanium, limestone, dolomite, sulphur, silver, tantalite, tungsten, rock and sea salt. The Brazilian reserves of iron ore alone are estimated at 50 billion tons, located in eastern Amazonia. Starting in 1985, exploitation to-date enables Brazil to satisfy world demand for iron for the next 500 years. This makes it the second-placed world producer and exporter of iron ore. Yearly production is some 215 billion tons, representing 20% of worldwide production. Moreover, Brazil has stocks of 208 billion tons of manganese, 2 billion tons of bauxite and 53 million tons of nickel[40].

## 3. Industry

With the installation of 200 large companies, 72 of which are publicly-owned, 21 privately- and 107 foreign-owned, Brazil has been able to demonstrate its expertise and know-how in the metallurgy sector, in oil and ethanol exploitation where it utilises the most advanced technology. Added to which it has processing installations for agro-food, textiles, cement and armaments, with 95% of production for export.

Since the 1970s and up until 2009, 7.9 million items have been manufactured each year; in the main, they comprise machines, vehicles, civil aircraft and agricultural machine tools, whose performance is described as the most advanced in the world.

Amongst its industries, the most advanced should be singled out: they are the naval shipyards, the pharmaceutical industry, together with those connected to the processing of mining and forestry products.

With particular reference to the oil industry, Brazil has considerable deposits that companies have been exploiting for some time. Additionally, with the discovery in May 2009 of important fields, 800 km long, 200 km wide and some 7000 m deep, its worldwide production capacity increased from 11.5 to 15.4 million barrels.

## 4. The energy sector

Brazil has some ten hydroelectric power plants including the largest in Latin America, namely that at Itaipu. This supplies the greatest part of the Brazilian territory, in addition to two neighbouring countries (Paraguay and Argentina). Brazil is a large producer of nuclear energy and is ranked sixth in the international market for enriched uranium for civil use. Apart from these two traditional energy sources, Brazil is currently recognised as having the best technology for the production of bioelectricity and ethanol derived from sugar cane.

---

[40]   Brazil, *Research journal of the Federal Government*, 2007.

The volumes produced by this sector are equivalent to 16% of the internal energy supply in Brazil. However, the production derived from sugar cane is in third position after that produced from petrol derivatives, which has a 37% share of public consumption.

With regard to the figures for the amount of energy produced by Brazil, the yearly average is as follows:

- 44.650 million barrels of oil;
- 6.7 million m³ of gas;
- 6.1 million tons of coal;
- 10 million kWh of electricity.

Two nuclear power plants (Angra1 and Agra2) should also be mentioned. It may be noted in this respect that Brazil has perfectly mastered the technique for nuclear combustion by enriched uranium, notwithstanding the ban imposed on it for the manufacture of atomic weapons.

## 5. Infrastructure

The Brazilian infrastructure is making great progress and this can be demonstrated by the following achievements:

- 8 million km of asphalt roads linking the four corners of the country, of which 2 million km are major roads;
- 5,018 km of railway track;
- 51 deep-water sea ports;
- 1500 airports (national and international) one of which has very heavy air traffic with a take-off and landing every five minutes.

## B. THE SECRETS OF BRAZIL'S SUCCESS

This amazing growth did not happen by chance. Even if some do think that world factors such as access to foreign capital and the rise in the price of raw materials did play a crucial part, it is generally agreed that Brazil's current success relies on good governance at political level together with a well-managed economy[41].

---

[41]   Cf. DE ONIS, J., "Brazil's Big Moment, A South American Giant Wakes up", *Foreign Affairs*, November-December 2008, vol. 87 n° 6, p. 110.

Added to which there is a sound educational system, built around the national and worldwide situation, an efficient banking system, a just and impartial legal system, good health care policies and the best terms for investment.

A question which might now be asked is: "what could DRC learn from Brazil's success and then how should it be put to good use? "

In the same vein, can be read: "Veritable geological giants, DRC just like Brazil has been blessed by nature, endowed with very rich mineral resources underground; both nations also have very similar climates and vegetation over their large expanse of land"[42].

And yet this country, categorised as "emerging", in which Congolese managers are employed, is not just a Latin American country. It is a Latin African country. It is the same with the United States, where President Barack Obama refers to himself as an "African American"[43]. Africans should capitalise on this situation as a fresh opportunity to cooperate with the Americas.

To make the comparison with the successful Brazilian experience, DRC should make a diagnosis and look for the same symptoms that the Brazilian economy also suffered over a long period. Then it should apply the same regime to treat the problems with courageous and difficult measures for each sector of our economy, on the understanding that the utmost attention be paid to agricultural production as well as to the production of consumer goods.

Just like Brazil, the revival of the development process in our country is closely bound up with the interaction of all mechanisms relating to these two sectors considered priorities. One of the ways to achieve this objective is to revive cooperation with Brazil, whose foreign policy offers specific advantages to all its friends in Africa engaged in the struggle against poverty, famine and under-development.

Also, DRC should strengthen its ties with this friendly country in order to quickly restore trade links which, of necessity, are conditional upon the resumption of the work of the important combined DRC-Brazil Commission for Cooperation. The planning of vitally important

---

[42]   *Ibid.*, p. 34.
[43]   OBAMA, B., *Dreams from my Father – A story of Race and Inheritance*, New York, Three Rivers Press, 2004, p. VII.

joint projects will depend on this body, in accordance with the agreements already signed by the two countries but not applied to-date. Moreover, using Brazil's example, DRC in response to the current world crisis should call upon its vast agricultural and ecological resources to consolidate a reprocessing industry to generate employment and revenues. Hence this would give a lesser priority to the more visible economy, dependent until now upon the meagre receipts from exported mining products. The aim would be to implement economically viable structures to improve social conditions and the wellbeing upon which our people undeniably depend.

## II. DRC is stagnating

Ever since 1960 and for reasons connected with its history, which has been interspersed with political trouble of various kinds, DRC, because of the failings of its politicians, has never had the time to give serious thought to the way forward for recovery.

It is also known that the country has only experienced relative peace since decolonisation, if indeed it is even true that colonisation has actually ended[44]. If there are indeed any endogenous[45] causes, it is nonetheless true that other causes are exogenous.

Madeline Albright recently admitted on leaving her post of Secretary of State that the "bitter rivalry between Hutus and Tutsis contributed to tip the vast DRC into war"[46]. And this ongoing rivalry heightens the strategic preoccupations which play a major role in DRC. The origins may well have been in 1816, just after the Congress of Vienna, when the British Captain Tuckey set out to find the source of the River Congo[47].

---

[44]   BRAECKMAN, C., *Vers la deuxième indépendance du Congo*, Kinshasa, Afrique Éditions, 2009, 267p.

[45]   N'KRUMAH, K., *L'Afrique doit s'unir*, Paris, Présence africaine, 1994, "The Congo declares itself an independent State in haste and for profit and immediately becomes a divisive battlefield encouraged by the imperialists (...) The Congo perhaps is the most striking example of the way in which dissent between tribes and political career aspirations have been exploited (...) to worsen these divisions" (pp. 203 and 221).

[46]   ALBRIGHT, M., *Mémoires*, Paris, Albin Michel, 2003, p. 549.

[47]   N'KANZA, Z.L. *Les origines du sous-développement politique au Congo-Belge. De Padroado à la Loi fondamentale, 1480-1960*, Kinshasa, Presses universitaires du Zaïre, 1985, p. 135.

This instability, one of the results of the bad creation of a State after Leopold's exploits, will be covered in the chapter on history. Henceforth, strategic information on the economy and the military situation must become a permanent fixation with DRC, with consideration given as to whether they deal with ensuring the stability of independent political institutions (1960), defending national sovereignty, territorial integrity and independence in order to restore the State's authority and the peace, or even prepare for possible armed aggression.

According to Professor Pierre AKELE ADAU, if we skim over the first 50 years of the country's independence, three main periods stand out.

"*Grosso modo*, it can be said that the twentieth century in Congo is characterised by a long period of sufferance during the actual decolonisation of the State, despite the sincerity of the struggle by the founding fathers of independence. It began negatively with the collapse and bankruptcy of the State and positively with the Nation's consolidation, revealing an affirmation of the Congolese identity by its heartfelt attachment to a fatherland founded upon a rich historical, cultural, political and social tradition with a common economy. The Nation is even more solid because it is based upon the blood of our heroes and martyrs, known and unknown, and the conviction of our vocation for peace but with strength (...) The 21$^{st}$ century should be a time to rebuild the State and democracy in Congo."[48]

When in 2006 with support and assistance from the international community, the Congolese agreed on the kind, form, organisation and functioning of power by adopting the Constitution of the Third Republic, promulgated on 18 February 2006 and then, on this basis, democratically established public institutions, multilateral partners encouraged the new public authorities to undertake an ambitious programme of governance, with due consideration given to the legitimate expectations of the population after the organisation of credible elections.

However, neither a programme for good governance nor a development programme could take shape without taking account of the major challenge of security and the defence of a country coveted by

---

[48] AKELE ADAU, P., "Défis de la gouvernance et de la démocratie en République démocratique du Congo", *Congo Afrique*, n° 439, November 2009, pp. 700-701.

predators on all sides because of its vast resources. At international level, the notion that the decline of a State as strategic as DRC poses a serious threat to international security has already been recognised. Thierry VIRCOULON even states that the decline of the Congolese State "constitutes an alarming phenomenon that undermines world-wide governance and increases regional instability"[49]. Thus it is clear that the rebirth of DRC as a regional power will depend on awareness of the need for defence and making borders secure.

Everyone knows that defence matters within the 192 UN Member States are shaped by military secrecy.

Even if some governments publish budgets for national defence in official journals and the fact that institutes specialising in matters of defence such as the International Institute of Strategic Studies (I.I.S.S.) in London and the Stockholm International Peace Research Institute (S.I.P.R.I.) publish some information in this area, they are at best only partial indications.

The same assessment can be made regarding the economy. In fact, the deep-seated crisis which is prevalent today in DRC also has its roots in longstanding problems dating from the colonial era. Hence when the Independent State of Congo was created, "gathering it all in" was the main way to build up capital. Nature provided enough products to satisfy the needs of the Congolese people as well as those in the metropolis.

With the demographic increases in Europe on the one hand, and the requirements for the industrialisation of Belgium on the other, the colonial power decided to impose some form of civilisation and forced labour on the Congolese, mainly through beatings.

Hence Congolese agriculture helped both the industrialisation of Belgium and the creation of industry in DRC. This system, though based on force, worked so well that the thriving Congolese economy enabled Belgium to be the only country in Europe to escape the economic crisis after the First and Second World Wars.

---

[49] VIROULON, T., "Ambiguités de l'intervention internationale en République démocratique du Congo", *Politique africain*, n° 98, June 2005.

In 1960, when our country became independent, DRC had the same level of growth as countries such as Canada, South Korea and South Africa, three countries nowadays irrefutably developed or developing.

## A. WHY IS DRC STAGNATING?

In 1960, DRC came into a world afflicted by size-related handicaps. It has wealth which is vast and diverse but which is exploited using experts, but not those from Congo.

So the Congolese are learning to administer a State with the dimensions of a continent, whilst discovering that their country is sitting upon wealth, one of the most fabulous in the world. They do not have the techniques nor the necessary know-how required to replace the Belgians caught up in the whirlwind of rebellions and secessions and who consequently felt the need to leave the country.

Neither the undertaking of management initiatives, nor those to restart or take them over have been achieved. In a short space of time, Congo is losing those who designed its economy and managed it on a day-to-day basis.

With a vandalised economy, together with leaders without any kind of proven expertise, DRC was, from the outset, condemned to move backwards.

History will recall however that in 32 years of rule, Mobutu did not manage to get Congo out of stagnation; in fact, it was the opposite, he hastened the decline.

Mobutu believed in the State as a provider. So after living on the reserves inherited from the Belgians and the First Republic, and incapable of any creative imagination, he resorted to the only solution that he believed was capable of reviving the country's economy. When it became "Zaire" in 1973, he took the most suicidal measure that a political power could sanction: snatching the possessions and all businesses belonging to foreigners to entrust them to Congolese people who had no proven experience in business management.

This course of action finished off an economy that was already comatose. Mobutu preferred, without maybe knowing it, to destroy what was already working, rather than trying to implement an audacious policy which would have enabled the country's economy to get back on its feet.

Moreover, the Congolese authorities and politicians were not concerned about the crucial matter of building up capital, which was underlying the prosperity amassed after the beatings stopped and the barriers and other restrictions imposed by the colonial power were removed. Instead of this, they considered their own political ambitions above all. The syndrome of creating political parties as an extension of ethnic or tribal origins dates back from this memorable period of independence. In this situation, those who lost elections or felt aggrieved took up arms. Those who were established in power and then were overthrown by force of arms joined the resistance.

The phenomenon of rebellion, which is a thorn in the flesh even today, also began during the same period. Instead of organising productive work and strengthening the State, Congolese leaders opted for the policy of making use of power, blind allegiance and sycophants. And the subservient elite were locked in step with the politicians, so much so that the only programme perfectly well executed, from independence to-date, is still that of the political repositioning, of power-sharing, often after useless and devastating wars, followed by talks, conclaves and conferences between Congolese politicians. There was no concern for the people who year-upon-year saw their living standards deteriorate. The governing powers, for their part, quickly found collaborators and offered them favours. The boss is and ought not to be contradicted; his word and his mistakes had the force of law.

In addition to political favouritism and despotism, this encouraged corruption, which it must be said has today reached worrying proportions in DRC, to the extent that after 50 years, the only result that can be frankly declared is to admit that the Congo, which on independence was listed as an emerging country, is now considered amongst the poorest countries on earth[50]. And the State, which can no longer honour its commitments towards its citizens and public concerns, becomes even more indebted, or even the largest debtor in the national economy. Its enterprises have been milked by their managers and political authorities. But when the milk runs dry, the State's representatives found a

---

[50]   Of interest is the study by the Reverend Father MINANI BIHUZO, R., *1990-2007, 17 ans de transition politique et perspectives démocratiques en RDC*, civil education paper, Kinshasa, CEPAS/RODHECIC, 2008.

new method: privatisation at any cost. Instances recorded showed that the public authorities were amongst the shareholders, sometimes with majority shareholdings, in those enterprises sold off cheaply. Bad governance is rampant and has become part of the structure of our economy. Shock therapy must be envisaged to make the State revert to social policies truly oriented towards improving the living standards of Congolese people.

The State's collapse causes anxiety, fear and despair in the minds of the people. The State's rehabilitation must take place within a new kind of social State, endowed with public authorities, motivated by the volition not only to make an honest living, to avoid social tensions or obtain personal favours from international donors, but also and mainly to re-establish social justice, to fight inequality and rebuild impartial cohesion[51].

These new social policies do not appear in any conceptual and theoretical vacuum; the same applies to our country; they should not be considered in isolation from the evolution of the national and international situation. We operate totally inside the framework of globalisation, where DRC has to refine its own model for development, adapted to its own particular situation.

This new form of development that should, we believe, depend upon a social liberalism where State regains its role as the regulator of public life and in the market place. This will enable us to avoid the sorry spectacle of a country where traffic jams comprising 4x 4 jeeps and luxury cars are increasing, caused by roads in a very bad state of repair and with insufficient public transport for average or poor Congolese.

When Joseph E. STIGLITZ considered the situation in Russia, he likened it to a symptom of sickness and not as a sign of health[52].

With respect to DRC, the distinction can be made between the construction of buildings, luxury apartments, villas and the total lack of social housing.

This situation makes it clear that national wealth, instead of being equally distributed, is concentrated in the hands of a small group of individuals representing, at most, two percent of the population.

---

[51]  Alternatives Sud, *op. cit.*
[52]  STIGLITZ, J. E., *La grande désillusion*, Paris, Fayard, 2002, p. 243.

DRC could warrant a thorough and detailed analysis because the lack of State intervention and badly applied liberalism has resulted in ruining all the aspirations of a totally neglected people. The country has been noticeably characterised over several decades by its predatory administration.

Although there were measures to liberate the exploitation of precious raw materials (diamonds and gold during the 1980s and the Second Republic), or the exploitation of the mining deposits held by large companies such as GÉCAMINES, KILOMOTO, MIBA, SOMINKI, of recent times, neither the State nor Congolese people have ever benefited from any of this.

The liberalisation of diamond and gold exploitation had two detrimental effects: the financial elite became scandalously rich and the poor, transformed into ordinary labourers or navvies to help fill the coffers of the rich, became even poorer.

Attracted by the illusion of easy money, young people and agricultural workers abandoned their schooling and the fields to invade the mines. The consequences are well known; the numbers in school keep on falling year-on-year; the rural exodus is getting worse and the mining provinces, previously the granaries of the Congo, have become importers of basic foodstuffs for their populations.

With regard to the large companies, the apparently praiseworthy idea of creating a mining registry was quickly shown to be a strategy to dispossess these enterprises of their wealth, sometimes to the benefit of individuals without the slightest intention of ever investing in the Congo.

Except for a few rare instances, the deposits of the Générale des Carrières et des Mines (GÉCAMINES), exploiting copper and cobalt in Katanga, and the Minière de Bakwanga (MIBA) in Eastern Kasai, a former world capital for the diamond industry, were sold for derisory prices. And the beneficiaries, according to the well-known practice, engaged in speculation, by simply trading the shares obtained at deliberately undervalued cost, on the stock exchanges of London, Toronto, Hong Kong, etc., at prices sometimes up to ten times their purchase price. Paradoxically, this system has shown that the holders of mining rights who did not remotely expect to make real investments in the country are subjected sometimes to excessive harassment, even to the extent of having their rights confiscated, thus exposing the State to lawsuits very unfavourable to the public purse.

This is why the Archbishop of Kinshasa, Mgr. Laurent MONSENGWO PASINYA, sounded the warning bell and invited all the Congolese authorities and the entire population, during the fiftieth anniversary of our country's independence, to make a retrospective and objective appraisal: "We must take stock of all the unworthy values which are stifling our society and which have kept on increasing to the point where now they are unmentionable"[53].

The rehabilitation of the State also implies an efficacious and dissuasive system for national defence. To demonstrate the importance of a defence system, General De Gaulle said in 1961: "A State and a government cannot keep their authority, nor prestige, if they are not seen by the people to be responsible for national defence."[54]. This declaration, nearly 50 years later, is still valid for DRC, which must of necessity establish a truly republican army.

## B. THE NEED TO ORGANISE CONGO'S DEFENCE

In spite of its nine frontiers, including the Atlantic coastline, DRC has not been able to equip itself with an army suited to the size of its territory, its demography, nor even its geostrategic position.

The various wars and rebellions with which its history has been beset from the start of independence until now have on each occasion broken up the embryonic defence force and then destroyed all attempts made to modernise it. If you then include the latest measure to collaborate and combine with rebel forces as well as other movements to defend themselves called "Maï-Maï", it is understandable how the Congolese army has become an incongruous juxtaposition of armed groups without any philosophical or historical connection between them.

In these circumstances, often the search for a precarious and superficial peace together with the selfish and undeclared interests which are at the basis of these kinds of groupings are not likely to stand the test

---

[53]  His Excell. Mgr MONSENGWO PASINYA, L., Homily for Easter 2010, "Ressuscités avec le Christ, recherchez donc les réalités d'en haut", pp. 11 and 12.
[54]  NOUZILLE, V., *Des secrets si bien gardés. Les dossiers de la Maison-Blanche et de la CIA sur la France et ses présidents, 1958-1981*, Paris, Fayard, 2010, p. 63.

of time, nor defend the fatherland or even to dissuade neighbours with malicious and hostile intent.

DRC needs an army of men and women who are trained, educated and well informed, a well-equipped and motivated army, and an army in time of peace to be diverted toward the goal of developing the country. It has to put up with an army without comradeship or team spirit, a reshuffled and disintegrating army.

In the same way, the forces of order and security, which have to support the national defence forces, should be reformed to become republican forces. The motivation and working condition aspects should not be ignored, for the time when a traffic policeman remains in the baking sun in Kinshasa from morning to night to control the capital's traffic jams should stop. Similarly, their barracks, the renovation of their canteens, health centres, and centres for continuous training and schools for their children should be remodelled.

Only in this kind of context can DRC regain its place in Africa and in the world arena and play a policing role in the Great Lakes Area and that of a military power to ensure a lasting peace in this region. This would be a real challenge for the Congolese government.

The DRC Parliament is considering a draft law to reform the army, a law that should offer a solution to the ills besetting our defence forces. But the law alone is not enough; strong determination and a firm political will are even more necessary to bring about the changes expected from a State being radically revived.

Generally speaking, Sub-Saharan Africa is experiencing an underperformance in defence, often attributed to a lack of logistical and financial means. These shortfalls often lead to the installation of an armed force bearing no relation to the number of inhabitants or even to the size of the land areas to be defended. From the incomplete information available to us at the moment, a few countries run counter to this trend: Angola which, after several years of civil war, is endowed with a really modern army and, to a lesser extent, Nigeria, which we recognise as fulfilling a mission to stabilise the entire West African region.

It is to be noted that South Africa is a special case, insofar as this country already has a real army inherited from the sad era when the country was run by the *apartheid* regime.

DRC is not exempt from the situation in Sub-Saharan African States, where there is no existing system for national defence. As far as this is concerned, the origin of this weakness can be found in the aftermath of the country's accession to independence.

The administrative organisation for national defence inherited from colonial times divided the country into three military regions:

– The first military region grouped together the Katanga Province (called the Shaba Province during the Second Republic) and the two Provinces in the Kasai (East and West);
– The second included the Provinces of Bandundu, the Lower-Congo (Lower Zaire during the Second Republic), Equator and the City of Kinshasa;
– The third comprised the Eastern Province (Upper Zaire during the Second Republic), the two Provinces in Kivu (North and South) and the Province of Maniema.

Currently, the country has eleven military regions, corresponding to the administrative provinces.

At the time of the country's accession to independence, the Congolese army did not include any high ranked officer, the highest ranked amongst the Congolese soldiers were the non-commissioned officers. So the gap left by the Belgian officers needed to be filled as quickly as possible. This is the source of the disarray we are experiencing today.

In these circumstances, the state of the Congolese armed forces very quickly deteriorated, as shown by the growing numbers of the incipient rebellions from the beginning of the First Republic. The central power could only be saved because of external UN intervention and that of mercenaries against the secession of Katanga and South-Kasai and also the Mulelist (movement founded by the revolutionary Pierre Mulele) rebellion in the North-East of the country.

When General Mobutu came to power, it was thought that the situation in the national army would improve. Unfortunately, this did not happen. In actual fact, as long as the regime in power did not face any armed conflict, nobody could have imagined the state of our armed forces. During the first (1977) then the second war of Shaba (1978), all the inadequacies of Zaire's armed forces were laid bare. Overall, the situation is deplorable; the pay is regularly misapropriated by the hierarchy, especially that of the troops on active duty. This leads to problems of a lack of motivation aggravated by logistical shortfalls. In almost all areas a lack of the means for the deployment and transport of troops, problems of shortages of arms, munitions and military uniforms, an obsolete or inexistent communications systems and no air cover are all to be deplored.

## C.  THE ESTABLISHMENT OF A NATIONAL DEFENCE FORCE

According to the statistics, there is one policeman for every 500 people in Europe. DRC with more than 70 million inhabitants is far removed from this ratio, like many other African countries. To emphasise the importance of the establishment of a defence force in DRC, you only have to look at the importance of the role that some authors and the great decision-makers had pre-ordained for DRC's security system.

Thus, as Henry KISSINGER noted "Belgian Africa (...) covers an area as large as Western Europe"[55]. It must be emphasised that this comment on the only African State studied is in the context of the "new and revised world order" after the increasingly marked assertions by the large countries of the South, the petrol kingdoms in the Gulf, the BRICS Group (Brazil, Russia, India, China and South Africa) as major players on the world stage, to the point where questions have been raised about the United States' perennial hegemony on earth and the viability of the financial and political international structures created in the wake of the Second World War, especially the UN Security Council, the International Monetary Fund and the World Bank, as well as the G7 Group of the seven most industrialised nations on earth established after the first petrol crisis (1973). Similarly, sight must not be lost of an appropriate reminder from one observer, well ahead of his time, Andre FONTAINE, according to whom vast Zaire, the ex-Belgian Congo, "the largest State in Africa" constitutes a protected hunting ground for the great capitalists"[56]. It is useful here to recall the opinion of the highest ranked official of the UN in Africa at the time, Layashi YAKER, who regretted that "Zaire (...) at the beginning of the 1970s had promised

---

[55]   KISSINGER, H., *Diplomatie*, Paris, Fayard, 1966, p. 736.
[56]   FONTAINE, A., *Un seul lit pour deux rêves – Histoire de la "détente", 1962-1981*, Paris, Fayard, 1981, p. 472.

to become a great economic power"[57]. The gamble is not lost if some paramount conditions are met such as those on defence and national security, provided that the decision-makers do not disagree.

In this vein, it is woeful, even revolting to note that DRC, with its large land mass and large population, does not have an army to suit its size. Yet it has been established that even in time of war, or in a post-conflict situation, a country can restructure its army and put a defence system in place just as Angola and other countries have done[58].

Yet even yesterday, officers from the armoured troops from 16 French-speaking African countries were trained at Mbanza-Ngungu (EFATBL) in the Lower-Congo and the Higher Military Academy of Kinshasa (CSM, created in 1969) saw the passing-out ceremony of newly qualified United States General Staff officers. It may be recalled that the Commando de Kotali training centre in the Equator Province trained the majority of the commandos in other Central African countries (Rwanda, Burundi, Tchad, Central African Republic, etc.). All of them, just like a large number of officers from African countries, were trained at the Kananga school for officers (EFO), at a time in 1975, according to Jean RYEMAN[59], when over 2500 Congolese officers were

---

[57]    YAKER, L., speech, in *The United Nations and development. The African situation*, conference 3-4 December 1993, Paris, Pedone, 1994, p. 163.

[58]    With regard to Angola, a model from which DRC could take inspiration, according to the American army's headquarters, this country has achieved its "Combat Performance" (Angola's population is estimated at 15 million inhabitants, less than a quarter of that in the Congo. It has a land area of 1,246,670 km². It has been independent since 11 November 1975. Its army has conducted operations in Sao Tomé, Congo-Brazzaville, Congo-Kinshasa and elsewhere): "It may be said that the Armed Forces for the Liberation of Angola, FAPLA, had substantially improved their capacity and performance. As a first step, the FAPLA started to develop its organisation and obtain the equipment worthy of a conventional army (...) Even though the navy had played a part in the military action, it was in fact the air force which had the decisive role. Only after the deployment of the anti-aircraft defence system and aircraft was Luanda able to mount and sustain a great offensive in the south, in the mid-1980s (...) The determination shown by Luanda and the improved capacities and performance of its armed forces were essentially part of the reasons for the South African army to negotiate its retreat from southern Angola." (Cf. Headquarters, Department of the Army, *Angola – a Country Study*, Washington, 1991, p. 231.

[59]    RYEMAN, J., *Le Monde diplomatique*, June 1975.

taking courses for in-depth training at: Fort Bragg, Annapolis, Sandhurst, Saint-Cyr, École royale des cadets, École royale militaire, Haiffa, Whimpoa, etc.

But bad administration in the army and nepotism were destroying Congolese armed forces. From decolonisation in 1960 to the overthrow of power in 1997, successive purges had converted the army into an instrument for a political regime, Mobutu's. Yet, however, this same army, when better managed, had intervened successfully in Tchad, for example, against the powerful Libyan army, and in Rwanda to repel the first attack of the FPR rebels against the Habyarimana regime in 1990.

Nepotism and unmerited appointments are like tumours eating away at the Congolese army and which must be cut out at any price. How can you explain that unworthy soldiers, without experience or the required training, were recruited to the rank of superior officers? Because of these repeated errors, our army is like an upside-down pyramid, where the very high proportion of superior officers in relation to lesser ranks does not conform to traditional standards.

Hence it is important that DRC which has ambitions to take part in forces to keep the peace in the Ivory Coast or in Haiti, for example, should reorganise its defence forces and its security arsenal, far removed from the current system of combining and superimposing former troops from diverse armed groups. The country must get itself a professional and republican army. By helping it towards this goal, the international community would ensure stability in the Sub-Region and the whole of Africa. Hence, instead of fearing the strengthening of the Congolese State and its army, it should be encouraged for obvious strategic reasons.

To do this, it is incumbent upon the Congolese authorities to show proof of their managerial skills and respect for commitments made.

In fact, the whole world knows that DRC has the world's greatest reserves of strategic minerals such as uranium, cobalt, niobium, Colombian tantalum, called "coltan", etc. The pillaging and plundering of these minerals are the major cause of the instability in the East of the country and the recurring wars that have caused at leave five million deaths over ten years. The international community should be called to account for this.

To maintain a zone without law and in a "low-level" war situation as it is called in security jargon, in this part of the country, could become dangerous in the long-term, even for those States beyond the Atlantic. If an international terrorist organisation should influence or seize a warlord controlling an area rich in strategic minerals, the danger will be there for everybody. This is why it must be made clear that the defence and secure borders of DRC are not just a national but also an international matter, especially in connection with military coopera-tion agreements.

## D. THE REVIVAL OF STRATEGIC AMBITIONS

Referring to the study by Crawford YOUNG and Thomas TUNER[60], Christopher CLAPHAM[61] summarises the agreement signed in March 1976 between the ex-Zaire and the (then) West German Orbital Trans-port and Raketen AG (OTRAG) as privatising diplomacy and selling off national sovereignty cheaply. This cannot be denied. Nevertheless, this deplorable episode shows, even if it is not needed, the strategic advan-tages that DRC clearly possesses. The country is the only African State which, in collaboration with a State from the North Atlantic, Germany, through the OTRAG company, had an experiment to put a rocket into space. Moreover, DRC is the only African country to have a nuclear reactor for research, used for peaceful purposes for agriculture and nuclear medicine by its national managers, trained at Mol (Belgium) or at the Commission for Atomic Energy (Paris) and based at the *Centre de Recherches et d'Études Nucléaires de Kinshasa* (CRENK).

Moreover, in its capacity as a Member State and party to the Treaty on the Non-Proliferation of Nuclear Weapons (NPT), DRC can develop its capacity in the sectors mentioned above. Hence, in 2009, the French President, Nicolas Sarkozy, made a tour of several African countries to make sure of his sources of supply for uranium and to promote the nuclear reactors produced by the French AREVA company. His visit to

---

[60] YOUNG, C. and TUNER, T., *The Rise and Decline of the Zaïrian State*, Madison, University of Wisconsin, 1985, pp. 387-388.
[61] CLAPHAM, C., *Africa and the International System. The Politics of State Survival*, Cambridge University Press, 1996, 252 p.

DRC culminated in the signing of an agreement on the exploration and exploitation of uranium by AREVA.

All things considered, the OTRAG affair which attempted two launches of space rockets in North-Katanga, though unsuccessful for technical reasons, demonstrates the geostrategic advantage that the Congolese airspace offers, as perceived by a great economic and financial power such as Germany.

Dependent upon a clearly defined programme and the determination of Congolese leaders, DRC is capable of gaining access, after Brazil, to the transatlantic sphere, to the exclusive club of space powers, with the ensuing positive implications. Far from imagining such a possibility as a threat, it should be considered as a reinforcement of technological capacity, useful to the region for telecommunications, telesurveyance, meteorology, etc.

Although this is true, an improvement to conventional forces is also necessary. This assumes the adoption of a law for its reorganisation, as mentioned previously, with a view to the gradual establishment of a new armed force, strong, disciplined, equipped, trained, with access to a social assistance structure and with an appropriate salary structure, located outside urban conurbations but in strategic areas.

This army would be composed of professionals, with an appropriate retirement pension, from all regions of the country, supervised by the best officers with qualifications from national and prestigious foreign military academies, thus making DRC a respected partner in international relations, especially between transatlantic countries.

Moreover, DRC, due to international technology transfers in particular, must gain advantage from its strategic natural resources used to develop the armament industries of the North, to create its own industries. There is at least one State in the region which has successfully met this challenge, the Republic of South Africa (RSA).

In this light, the proposal for a permanent seat for DRC in the Security Council of the United Nations must be revived. This subject was debated at the time when the RSA, Egypt, Nigeria and even Ghana, Kenya and Senegal were claiming admission to the UN Security Council, the true world government. The preceding arguments for admission used by the first generation of permanent members may be spotlighted; France defeated and in capitulation, was set free by the

United States of America and Great Britain, whilst China was occupied by Japan on one hand (Manchuria) and on the other facing a general-ised civil war. E. McWHINNEY could then maintain that "of the Five Powers on whom the Charter conferred the privilege of veto (...), there were three countries which were only great world powers by virtue of convention or a legal device"[62]. No doubt this will happen again soon.

When you know that on two occasions, during two world crises (the Falklands, 1982, and Kuwait, 1991), DRC chaired the UN Security Council, you may justifiably wonder for how much longer it will continue to drag behind, when in Sub-Saharan Africa, Nigeria excluded, it possesses the highest concentration of human resources, special-ists in civil, military, scientific, technical, commercial, administrative and international domains, and who have contributed to the teaching (including that on economics and business management) at universities in several African countries.

In this connection and according to recent information (DRC diplo-matic and consular missions in South Africa, Rwanda and Burundi), over 2000 Congolese doctors work in South Africa and half of the teachers in neighbouring Rwanda are Congolese. Account must also be taken of all the Congolese scientific leading lights dispersed throughout the West and elsewhere.

This brain drain has been compounded by the deterioration in social structures and the Congolese economy, the crumbling Adminis-tration, insecurity and political restraint.

Congolese decision-makers should consider the special case of Rwanda. In fact and due to the good organisation of the Rwandan educational system, where teacher motivation is the main government concern, Congolese university professors, particularly those from Goma and Bukavu, prefer to emigrate to Rwanda and then become visiting professors at universities in their own country.

The case of Southern Africa also speaks for itself. The majority of engineers and doctors from GÉCAMINES in Katanga decided to emigrate to southern Africa and to South Africa in particular. If nothing is done about it, then DRC risks losing its intellectual elite.

---

[62]    McWHINNEY, E., *Les Nations unies et la formation du droit*, Paris, Pedone, 1986, p. 111.

The realisation of these strategic ambitions will once again result from good management of the country's sovereign interests by its leaders, whilst remaining faithful to the principles on which its foreign policy is founded, in particular being a good neighbour and opening up our country to the outside world.

## E. NEED TO COMPENSATE FOR LACK OF A BUFFER[63] ZONE

Except for its 41-km maritime coastline, DRC does not possess a buffer zone behind which the national sanctuary would be protected. Its coastal area does however enable a naval base to be established. It also enables the maritime buffer zone to extend to the high seas, especially by allowing submersible missiles to make the first and most destructive strike. It is still true however that the lack of a protective buffer for a land surface of 2,345,000 km$^2$, bordering nine States, does warrant the development of a national industry for ballistic missiles, as in the South African Republic. The latter has missiles able to reach targets located thousands of kilometres away from the Simonstown base.

Ultimately, the position and the strategic challenge of DRC are perfectly obvious from various points of view. If the Congolese land area is equally well compatible with the Congolese State and with the Congolese nation, shaped by years of oppression and hope, facts must be faced. The idea that the national sanctuary creates its own strategic space which should dissuade secondary and smaller States from becoming military aggressors, directly or by using mercenaries, is only in the mind of DRC. The recent history of a country laid waste by more than three decades of tyranny shows the limits of this kind of assessment.

A geostrategy is the only way to achieve a study of the principles relating to its land. History and culture are the main bases for man's development

---

[63] Buffer to protect national security.

CHAPTER III

# Historical and socio-cultural information

If history is a strategic discipline in social science, it teaches all about the past and partly explains the present. It enables us to anticipate the future. Contrary to the historical chronicle of the conqueror, persistently defended to-date, Africa, and within the continent, DRC has probably had its own history since the origins of humanity.

## I. Ancient African populations
## and emergence of original Congolese civilisations

### A. ANCIENT AFRICAN POPULATIONS

As held by Cheikh ANTA DIOP, "there is every indication from the beginning, in the prehistoric and higher Paleolithic period, that Negroes were predominant. They remained supreme during historical periods over thousand of years of civilisation in technical and military matters."[64]

Andrei GROMYKO, USSR Minister of Foreign Affairs for 28 years (1957-1985), recalls that "Africa had its own civilisation, long before the colonialists arrived. In fact, as science teaches us, Africa is where man took his first steps (...) But the ancient African States were incapable of resisting pressure from the Europeans who arrived armed with a bible and a gun (...) Fatally weakened by the negro slave trade, the continent's development was held back even more during the era of colonialism"[65].

---

[64] ANTA DIOP, C., *Antériorité des civilisations nègres: mythe ou vérité historique?* Paris, Présence africaine, 1967, p. 14.
[65] GROMYKO, A., *Mémoires*, Paris, Belfond, 1989, p. 256.

## B. THE EMERGENCE OF ORIGINAL CONGOLESE CIVILISATIONS

The Vice President of the International Court of Justice mentions the "Kivu" in one of his studies, as one of several ancient African States.[66].

In particular, Fouad AMMOUN highlights "the civilisations of the Great Lakes, where traces of roads, irrigation canals, dikes and aqueducts, of an admirable technical quality are to be found"[67]. Briefly, quoting Raimondo LURAGHI: "Hence at the moment the Portuguese arrived, a unique history had already been unfolding over centuries and millennia from the Sahara Desert to South Africa; a history of civilised people comparable with those in the great empires of Latin America or Europe during the most remarkable periods in Antiquity and the Middle Ages."[68].

With regard to the peoples of the Congo, scientists have considered the pygmies, or Batwa, Tuides or Négrilles, to be the first inhabitants in this area[69], especially in the equatorial forest, the Ituri or Kivu regions. Recently, David RENTON et al., taught us that "it was probably during the fifth dynasty (in 2500 BC) that the Egyptians had knowledge of pygmies, when an expedition had brought back a "dwarf" from the Punt country. Pharaoh Pepi III of the sixth dynasty (about 2300 BC) had images of pygmies drawn on his tomb".[70]

Around 200 BC, the Bantus, to escape the drought, emigrated from the mouth of the River Niger to the Congolese territory from the South to the North, from the West to the East, though it is not necessary to describe the various migrations in detail. David RENTON et al. cover them in great detail[71].

---

[66]  AMMOUN, F., Separate opinion in attachment to the consultative advice of 21 June 1971 in the matter of the *Legal consequences for States of the continued presence by South Africa in Namibia (South-west Africa) notwithstanding resolution 276 (1970) of the Security Council*, International Court of Justice, *Collection*, 1971, pp. 25-86.

[67]  *Ibid.*, p. 86.

[68]  *Ibid.*

[69]  MBWAKI, N. *Histoire, Atlas de la République du Zaïre*, Paris, Editions Jeune Afrique, 1978, p. 24.

[70]  RENTON, D. *et al.*, *The Congo, Plunder and Resistance*, London, Zed Books, 2007, p. 7.

[71]  *Ibid.*

Incidentally, the anthem of national freedom against the colonial occupier, the "Debout Congolais" (Stand up you people of Congo), is perhaps an inaugural text to commemorate the Congolese population and their steadfast identity. In carrying out the task of portraying his people, the Congolese historian, Isidore NDAYWEL, goes further: "It might be said that destiny is keen to guarantee a minimum of continuity"[72] for Congolese people, "the point of departure for any requirement for unity was controlled by elements even in the environment"[73]. Such unity goes back to the "most distant age (...) practically to the beginning of humankind"[74]. Therefore "it must be realised that the unity of Congo is not an artificial creation from the colonial era"[75]. This does not mean that there is any intention at all to remain oblivious to the contributions made by individual or collective colonial regimes experienced in Congo (ISC, or Independent State of Congo, and the Belgian Colony) or even less those of the neo-colonial politicians who ensured the continuity of the former regimes.

When Honoré VINCK conducted a passionate review of this key paper by Isidore NDAYWEL, he did not hesitate to reproach him for being a "nationalist"[76]. Neither VINCK, nor MICHELET in France, could be considered as such. It would be interesting to know whether H. VINCK recognised the accuracy of the study by David RENTON *et al.* who maintain: "Congo's history began well before contact with Europeans, who claimed to be the first to have "discovered" the country. Archaeological findings enabled some writers to describe the Sangoa people, who lived in the Central African area 50,000 years ago. They used knives and scrapers and travelled between caves lit by fire."[77]

Other archaeological findings bear witness to the far-distant cultural past of Congo. In 1950, Jean De Heinzelin, a researcher at the Belgian Royal Institute for Natural Science, led an expedition to excavate in Ishango. On a fossil ledge by the Semlike River, where it enters

---

[72]  NDAYWEL, I., *Histoire du Zaïre*, Louvain-la-Neuve, Duculot, Paris, ACCT, 1997, pp. 253-256.
[73]  *Ibid.*
[74]  *Ibid.*, pp. 776-777.
[75]  *Ibid.*, p. 256.
[76]  VINCK, H., Bibliographical reviews, *Annales Aequatoria*, vol. 18, 1997, p. 594.
[77]  RENTON, D., *et al.*, *op. cit.* p. 7.

Lake Edward, he dug up white quartz tools, harpoons, shells and the thereafter famous "Ishango stick". This reshaped bone, dating back 18,000 years from the present, has a series of notches engraved in a regular pattern. In fact, on three of its surfaces, various sequences of transversal incisions can be seen. Many of the researchers who have examined this stick came to the conclusion that it was a mathematical instrument which then became the oldest known object of the type known. Even though caution must prevail, the arithmetical connection theory makes it difficult to ignore the notion that this indicates some kind of mathematical instrument[78].

The time will come when the elation of the patriot feeling of the Congolese over a long time-span will be revealed, when other facts and future opinions become known.

## C. THE CONSTELLATION OF FORMER CONGOLESE STATES

Several independent political groupings have been established ever since the 13th century on the actual territory of Congo.[79] These include the Kongo kingdom, founded in 1275 by Nimi-A-Lukeni and the Loango kingdom, created in the 15th century and which cooperated with the Kongo kingdom. The Bayaka[80], Yaka, Gaga or Jaga[81] empire existed East of the Kongo kingdom, according to various authors. In the same era, the Luba kingdom under the rule of Kongolo came into being. The Lunda empire was established in the 17th century by Yamvu Nawej. The last-named came to the throne with the title Mwat yamv. Further south, the M'Siri kingdom was at its peak in the 19th century. It heroically resisted the colonial invasion until the death of the king[82].

---

[78]  http://www.naturalsciences.be/expo/old8ishango/fr/exhibition/ishango8presse.pdf.
[79]  The glaring errors of some African specialists do not matter. (We can agree with COQUERY-VIDROVITCH, *Afrique noire. Permanences et ruptures*, Paris, Payot, 1985, pp. 178 and 424, who situates the Congolese area (ex-Zaire) of Maniema in "Lower-Zaire" [Lower-Congo].)
[80]  MBWAKI N., *op. cit.*, pp. 24-27.
[81]  RENTON, D., *et al.*, *op. cit*, p. 14.
[82]  *Ibid.* Its territory can be considered to stretch from "the Atlantic Ocean, along the Ogoué (Gabon) towards Stanley Pool, through the Batéké Plain, up to Kwango and all of northern Angola".

It is also important to point out that in this geographical area a Bemba empire began to take shape towards the end of the 18th century under pressure from the Lunda[83]. The existence of the Kazembe kingdom and the Yeke[84] empire are also recorded. What remains to be said about the Mongo people who, up to now, have remained in the deep forest of the Congo and who have inhabited the forest area east of Mbandaka at least since the first century of our era, since when they have left their mark as hunters and cultivators of yams[85]?

Additionally, two kingdoms clearly stand out in the North, deep in the forest: the kingdoms of Azande and Mangbetu. It is likely that other independent groups existed that the African oral tradition has forgotten, or that the colonial European ethnocentrism chose to ignore or even reduced them to the level of local African tribes.

Nonetheless, and with a view to renewing transatlantic ties, a re-examination of the Kongo kingdom would be necessary. Well before the invasion and the occupation of Congo by the Belgian colonialists, the Congolese, for four centuries previously, had had contacts with the European settlers along the coast[86]. It should be made clear that the Congolese in question were part of the Congolese population living along the Atlantic coast. But at the same time we must recognise that this community was "the largest kingdom in the area"[87]. The transatlantic relationship was created by the Kongo.

Whatever the case, all these independent communities were carried away by the groundswell which swept over Africa during the colonial era.

## D.  THE LONG COLONIAL AND NEOCOLONIAL NIGHT

Jules MICHELET may well have written, "wiping out a world at one stroke, and remaking it at another, a particular incurable sickness in the human mind"[88]. We would willingly agree that such a practice is a path-

---

[83]   RENTON, D., *et al., op. cit*, p. 15.
[84]   *Ibid.*
[85]   *Ibid.*, p. 8.
[86]   KAKÉ, I. *et al. Conflit belgo-zaïrois*, Paris, Présence africaine, 1990, p. 41.
[87]   *Ibid.*
[88]   MICHELET, J., quoted by FONTAINE, A., *op. cit.*, p. 19.

ological problem. But whether it is considered incurable is a matter for biomedical science. We know that the Congolese endured two successive colonialist systems: one private, the pseudo-Independent State of Congo, the other public, the Belgian Congo. It is necessary to mention them briefly in the current context.

## E. LEOPOLD'S FICTITIOUS "INDEPENDENT STATE OF CONGO"

The current boundaries of DRC were recognised at the conclusion of the Berlin Conference in 1885. On 1 August 1885, King Leopold II of Belgium, assumed the sovereignty of what was called the Independent State of Congo (ISC) through the African International Association (AIA), whose evolution is covered hereafter.

However, it is known that the atrocities inherent in the relentless exploitation system of red rubber were such that they caused outrage amongst the international community of the day and obliged the King of the Belgians to renounce his own personal regime in Congo due to the negative aspects which were weighing heavily against him.

We owe the following analysis to Félicien CATTIR, "the Independent State of Congo is nothing but a colonising State (...) It is hardly a State, it is a commercial enterprise."[89]. Whilst one American president proclaimed that "Congo business is business"[90]. One historian believed that the 25 years of Leopold's rule "definitely figured as the gloomiest, most dramatic and bloodiest period in the Congo's history"[91]. Although very indulgent concerning Leopold II, B. EMERSON describes him as follows, "Leopold was doubtless no worse than many others. The way in which he did outdo everybody else was by his cruelty, insensitivity and his spitefulness (...) the most serious charge that may be levelled against him was that he obstinately refused, although he was completely well informed and could have put an end to the atrocities committed in the African state that he personally and absolutely controlled (..) he was hard-hearted and merciless."[92]

---

[89]   See EMERSON, B., *op. cit.*
[90]   MBOKOLO, E., " Le Congo, Colonie modèle", in *Conflit belgo-zaïrois, Fondements politiques, économiques et culturels*, Paris, Présence africaine, 1990, p. 18.
[91]   *Ibid.*, p. 11.
[92]   EMERSON, B., *op. cit.*, p. 66.

But when dealing with renewed transatlantic relations, Leopold's abominable acts are relevant when considering how to repair the damage caused by colonialism and the subsequent neo-colonialism. Additionally, the edifying research works of Daniel VANGROENWEGHE[93], Adam HOCHSCHILD[94], M. EWANS[95] and David RENTON *et al.*[96] are recommended for reading. In this context, it is important to emphasise Leopold II's determination and guile behind recognition of Congo as a country. Bismarck, the German Chancellor, moreover described Leopold II's position in a "confederation of free States" as "deceptive" and "unbelievable"[97].

Succumbing to international pressure in 1908, Leopold II yielded up his colony to the Belgian State and it only became independent in 1960, after 80 years as a colony.

## F.  RECOGNITION OF "AFRICAN INTERNATIONAL ASSOCIATION" OR "INTERNATIONAL ASSOCIATION OF CONGO" BY UNITED STATES OF AMERICA

The first instance of international acceptance of Leopold II's designs for Congo was by the American President, Chester A. Arthur. The US Minister for Belgium, General Henry Shelton Sanford, carried out some successful lobbying to achieve this objective. Leopold II requested Arthur for "the official announcement that the government of the United States would hold out a flag of friendship (...) with golden stars which then blew over 17 outposts, numerous territories, seven steamboats and was engaged in a civilising mission for the Association and a population of several million men"[98]. Sanford "confided (...) to the president and to all those he met in the capital" that "Leopold's great civilising task (...) bore a great resemblance to the munificent mission achieved by the United States (...) in Liberia (...) to where freed Amer-

---

93   VANGROENWEGHE, D., *Du sang sur les lianes. Léopold II et son Congo*, Brussels, Didier Hatier, 1986, 293 p.
94   HOCHSCHILD, A., *Les fantômes du roi Léopold*, Paris, Belfond, 1998, 439 p.
95   EWANS, M., *European Atrocity, African Catastrophe: Leopold II, the Congo Free State and Its Aftermath*, London, Routledge, 2002.
96   RENDON, D. *et al.*, *op. cit.*, p. 243.
97   HOCHSCHILD, A., *op. cit.*, p. 105.
98   *Ibid.*

ican slaves had emigrated as early as 1820 and which was rapidly to become an independent African country"[99].

This example had been cleverly chosen because it was not the American government that had settled former slaves in Liberia, but a private company, similar to Leopold's International Association for Congo[100]. In addition, "in his letter to President Arthur, Leopold promised that American citizens would be free to buy things in Congo and that American goods would be exempt over there from customs duties"[101]. Furthermore, "did these independent States under the generous protection of the Association not represent a kind of United States of Congo? "[102]. The President inserted in his annual message to Congress a text only slightly rewritten for him by Sanford" which was, "The rich and highly populated valley of Congo has been opened up by a company called the African International Association, whose president is the King of the Belgians (...) Large expanses of territory have been made over to the Association by native chiefs, roads have been built, steamboats have been put to float on the river and the basic elements of a State established (...) under a flag offering freedom of trade and prohibiting the slave trade (...)"[103].

For Senator John Tyler Morgan of Alabama, former Brigadier General in the Confederate Army and President of the Senate Committee for Foreign Affairs, "frightful of the spectre of millions of freed slaves and their descendants nurturing threatening dreams of equality"[104], "Leopold's new State was a present from heaven (...) And would the Congolese not show their eagerness to trade with the United States, if the Americans that they met had the same colour skin as themselves? Besides, would Congo not become a market for the surplus cotton from the South? Africa was, he assured the Senate shortly afterwards, ready for the Negro as the Garden of Eden was certainly ready for Adam and Eve (...) We will find the best members of the negro race

---

[99] *Ibid.*, pp. 97-98.
[100] *Ibid.*
[101] *Ibid.*
[102] *Ibid.*
[103] *Ibid.* p. 95.
[104] *Ibid.*, quoting Morgan.

in the Congo Basin, and the American Negro (...) can there find scope for his endeavours"[105].

The picture that Stanley painted of the areas he saw was idyllic. "In this vast virgin land, there is enough potential that, if exploited, it could produce half a million tons of rice per year, but also wheat, sugar, yams, potatoes, millet and sweet-corn *ad infinitum*. Even the slopes of these mountains that protect the plain against the cold, violent wind of the south Atlantic would allow the profitable cultivation of tea, coffee, sorghum and other spices."[106]

Sanford, Leopold II's emissary, "arranged for the New York Chamber of Commerce to pass a Resolution in the Senate endorsing the recognition of Leopold's Association by the United States"[107] The act of recognition, presented by Secretary of State Frelinghuysen, was drawn up as follows, "The United States' Government announces that it understands and approves of the human and generous objectives of the International Association of Congo which administers, as indeed it is already doing, the interests of the free States, established over there, and gives the order to United States officers, both on land and at sea, to recognise the flag of the African International Association as that of a friendly government."[108].

The Resolution was voted in April 1884 (on the 11 April according to EMERSON[109] and on the 22nd to HOCHSCHILD[110]). Whatever was published elsewhere, "recognition by the United States gave new life to the Association", in the opinion of Henry Morton Stanley[111], or John Rowland as was his real name. Another example is the acceptance of a

---

[105]  *Ibid.*, p. 101.
[106]  See, RENTON, D., *et al. op. cit.*, p. 20.
[107]  *Ibid.*, p. 101. "Articles favourable to the philanthropic activities of the King appeared in the major American newspapers, encouraged, as was the custom at that time, by bribes that were discretely given to them by Sanford. His widespread campaign is probably the most extensive lobbying ever conducted in Washington in the name of a foreign government during the 19th century", *ibid.*
[108]  *Ibid.*, p. 102.
[109]  EMERSON, B., *op. cit.*, p. 105.
[110]  HOCHSCHILD, A. *op. cit.*, p. 101. Likewise for Zala L. NKANZA, *op. cit.* p. 147.
[111]  HOCHSCHILD, A. *op. cit.*, p. 102.

preferential right in favour of France "at the same time as Sanford was getting ready to return in triumph to Belgium".[112]

Scarcely "two months after the end of the Conference, a vessel from the United States navy, the "Lancaster", appeared at the mouth of the Congo and fired a 21-gun salute in honour of the blue flag with the golden stars"[113].

From 15 November 1884 to 26 February 1885, when the European negotiations culminating in the signing of the Act of Berlin came to an end "not one single African was sitting at the table in Berlin"[114]. This was the conspiracy of the century against Africa, the consequences of which are still being felt.

## 1. American interest in recognising A.I.A.

The preceding developments give sufficient indication of the reasons which led the Government of the United States of America to recognise Congo from April 1884, which is six months prior to the opening of the European conference on 15 November 1884, held to carve up Africa. With respect to the continuing economic and commercial interests of America and other Western Atlantic countries, a reminder of these historical and current data is necessary. When, in March 2008, the New York press accuses the Chinese, who are also developing a substantial volume of trade in goods and services with the United States, as being "New Colonialists"[115] especially with regard to Congo, this confirms the permanent American interest in the country.

As history constantly repeats itself, current leaders have to understand that the transatlantic relations envisaged, according to the North American standpoint, are linked to trade and particularly to maritime trade[116].

Furthermore, Colette BRAECKMAN, when evoking a total or partial failure of Sino-Congolese contracts, which are viewed from the

---

[112]  *Ibid.*

[113]  *Ibid.*, p. 105.

[114]  *Ibid.* p. 108.

[115]  *The Economist*, 15-21 March 2008, pp. 12-14.

[116]  To reward his good and loyal services, « Sanford will receive a large concession in the Congo, where he will establish a commercial firm, *The Exploratory Sanford Expedition*", see Zala L. NKANZA, *op. cit.*, p. 147.

Western point of view as the Congolese Government showing some ingratitude regarding "only Europeans"[117], explains that the Western companies have nothing to fear from a possible rivalry when Chinese companies suddenly appear[118].

## 2. Enduring Western interests

Today and somewhat belatedly, opinions are being increasingly voiced in the West to recognise the responsibility of this part of the world in DRC's stagnation and the need for a renewed independence. By way of an example, let us quote Colette BRAECKMAN who mentions in her book the need for a "second independence for Congo"[119].

For some time now, prominent political figures[120], from universities[121], and some other foreign observers have been denouncing the disorganised decolonisation of the Belgian Congo. In actual fact, this is generally the case with decolonised African countries[122].

A quick look at the DRC's history shows that Congolese people organised themselves after their own fashion, although simply, in the period preceding colonisation and before the Whites arrived in their territory. They lived as separate nations which today form part of the national sanctuary; these very nations cooperated in one way or other with the foreign powers.

---

[117]   BRAECKMAN, C. *Vers la seconde indépendance du Congo, op. cit.*, p. 184.
[118]   *Ibid.*
[119]   *Ibid., p. 267.* The title refers to the study by A.A.J.VAN BILSEN, *Vers l'indépendance du Congo et du Ruanda-Urundi*, Kraainem, 1959, see also VAN BILSEN "Un plan de trente ans pour l'émancipation de l'Afrique belge", *Les dossiers de l'action sociale catholique*, n° 2, February 1956, pp. 83-111.
[120]   See N'KRUMAH, K., *op. cit.*, p. 221. In dealing with "neo-colonialism in Africa", he believed that "the Congo is perhaps the most striking example of this".
[121]   See KI-ZERBO, J., preface to the work of A. A. DICKO, *Journal d'une défaite. Autour du referendum du 28 septembre 1958 en Afrique noire*, Paris, L'Harmattan, 1992, p. XIV.
[122]   OGINDA, O., *Not Yet Uhuru*, Nairobi, East African Educational Publishers, Foreword by Kwame Nkrumah, 1967, p. 256, "*Throughout Kenya's colonial period the colonial government aided by the settlers, concentrated on infiltrating the nationalist movement and creating and encouraging divisions and splits within. The strategy was to place in power in Kenya those elements that would be favourably inclined to Britain and would safeguard her economic and military interest.*"

But the African slave trade and colonisation radically changed the course of Congo's history, by taking the best of its sons and daughters and making a slave of its economy.

Nevertheless, colonisation had put down solid roots on which to create a prosperous society, had it not been for the badly managed and the practically irresponsible administration of the Congolese leaders.

Is it possible to keep on accusing the colonisers fifty years after independence, without the Congolese making their own critical self-assessment?

The Congolese must make sure to change the situation because they have the capacity and the means, instead of continually blaming it on the Belgians. Although saying this does not exonerate the effects of colonisation.

It would seem that if there was to be referendum on the question of a return to Belgian colonisation, a large part of the Congolese population would answer "yes", given the very appreciable regression in the current standard of living compared with that in 1960, together with a marked deterioration in the administration, the dilapidated state of the infrastructure, the destruction of the economic fibre, and educational and health care systems.

But we must not be defeatist, particularly when the Congolese possess the required resilience in their society and culture to bounce back.

This historical reminder is necessary because those who have been successful in the past can succeed in the present and the future. A population which does not face up to its own history is condemned to stagnate, regress, and even disappear. To follow up this reminder, a look at the cultural and sociological dimensions of the DRC is also warranted.

## II. Cultural and sociological dimensions [123]

### A. THE SOCIOLOGICAL MAKE-UP

The sociological field is particularly sensitive. An observation of African society reveals groups labelled "ethnic", "tribal" or "ancestral", etc. To understand these notions is to understand African society.

According to Bruno CRINE-MAVAR, "the name 'ethnic group' is now reserved to each grouping of human beings who share the same cultural heritage although the groups included in it are not necessarily subject to the same political authority"[124]. As mentioned by this author, "the tribe is to the ethnic group what the atom is to the molecule"[125]. In other words, the ethnic group is comprised of tribes. However, and as indicated by Catherine COQUERY-VIDROVITCH, first of all the notion of ancestry has to be grasped to then allow an understanding of the ethnic group. Ancestry would correspond to a "group descending from the same non-mythical ancestor, i.e. children, relatives, great-nephews and dependents, etc."[126]. It is "the entire ancestry which forms the ethnic group, whose cultural identity is confirmed by the recognition of a common mythical ancestor and is confirmed by an unmistakeable linguistic community"[127].

Nevertheless, the historian would admit the "derogatory connotation" of the word "tribe", resulting from "its abusive use during the colonial era"[128]. And "ethnic group" itself "is no less worthy of being treated with care because it has become more exaggerated and inflexible because of the ethnologists"[129]. In conclusion, scientists note that some "very contemporary analyses cast doubts upon the relevance of

---

[123] In the accepted complete meaning, the measurement gauge for culture encompasses sociological aspects. However, to obtain a better understanding, the option of dealing separately with these concepts and to change their order has been raised.

[124] CRINE-MAVAR, B., *Ethnies et langues. Atlas de la République du Zaïre*, Paris, Éditions J.A., 1978, p. 28.

[125] *Ibid.*

[126] COQUERY-VIDROVITCH, C., *op. cit.*, p. 74.

[127] *Ibid.*

[128] *Ibid.*

[129] *Ibid.*

the very African concept of Ethnic Group which is, mainly and always, a historical perception liable to substantial evolution"[130].

However, we would mention some ethnic groups which, although very different from one another, are included in the same linguistic community. This is the case for example with the Lulua and the Luba in both Kasai[131] provinces.

If, during the period of Africa's independence, the above author observes something of a balance in the entire culture, in a historic and collective context and recognisable as such, she comments that during the colonial era, "the ethnic group was mostly fabricated for the purpose of control, not just administrative and political, but also religious"[132]. Should we not have feared a worse situation in the neo-colonialist era? Ethnic conflicts, according to the dominant media, occur all over Sub-Saharan Africa. During that time in 2006, in the City of Kinshasa, when countless Congolese, scarcely twenty years of age, to be included on the electoral register, had to ask their parents about their tribe, their ethnic group, their original community, we would have been inclined to share the assumption that the ethnic group is a sociological construction, subject to the people's historic evolution.

Globally, the existence of ethnic groups in Congo cannot be denied, nor even the manipulation for undeclared aims to which this sociological category is currently being subjected, just like the lack of precise limitations on the ethnic group concept.

Although he had otherwise made a demarcation between ethnic group and tribe, Bruno CRINE-MAVAR seems to favour a study of tribes. He categorically states, "There is no doubt that their total number is close to the half-thousand."[133]. This estimation however contrasts with the final assessment when he names 365 Congolese tribes.

---

[130] *Ibid.*, p. 75.
[131] Fearful of the unavoidable decolonisation of the Congo, the Belgian colonial authorities artificially stimulated the tribal war between the members of two tribes, Lulua and Luba, who were living peacefully together up until the eve of independence
[132] COQUERY-VIDROVITCH, C., *op. cit.*, p. 127.
[133] CRINE-MAVAR, B. *op. cit.*, p. 28.

For his part, Léon De SAINT-MOULIN presents some "ethnic groups and tribes mixed together per territory"[134] in Congo, which makes a total of 280. Not only was the study made at a time of political controversy but furthermore, it is the work of a university missionary. Has he managed to escape the criticism of historians like Catherine COQUERY-VIDROVITCH about the negative contribution of the missions in this field? On the one hand, it would not be possible with complete scientific rigour for any confusion between ethnic groups and tribes. The two sociological categories are hardly identical. Distinguishing one from the other is a scientific necessity. On the other hand, counting altogether no more than 280 ethnic groups and tribes could change the sociological chemistry. There would probably be many more of them. Moreover, proposing a definition of ethnic group as a "construction, with different origins but not systematic"[135] leaves the reader to expect more information. Defining the phenomenon is still a very incomplete undertaking.

Besides, it is not at all certain that the limits of state frontiers absolutely agrees with the tight lines drawn between ethnic groups, such as the Bemba and Lunda in Angola and Zambia, and the Bakongo in DRC, Angola and Congo Brazzaville. Likewise, do the administrative limits within States correspond to a precise localisation of ethnic groups? It would be presumptuous to state this categorically. Consider the situation of the Pende ethnic group; not only is it dispersed between the Gungu and Idiofa territories, in the Kwilu district of the Bandundu province, but furthermore the sociological group concerned has been split between the two provinces of Bandundu and West Kasai since the anti-colonialist insurrection of 1930-1931. This situation has been repeated with the examples of the Yansi occupying four territories, namely, Bagata, Bulungu, Kenge and Masi-Manimba, which are in the Kwilu and Kwango districts, and the Bashi people who occupy the Kabare, Walungu and Uvira territories, and the Lega who occupy the Mwenga and Shabunda territories in the South-Kivu province and the Pangi and Punia territories in the Maniema province.

---

[134]  De SAINT-MOULIN, L., « Conscience nationale et identités ethniques. Contribution à une culture de paix », *Congo-Afrique*, December, 1998, pp. 587-622.
[135]  *Ibid.*, p. 587.

At least this outline of the sociological mix which makes up the Congo demonstrates the pluralism and affinities of the groups of people living there. Hence it is possible to draw a parallel between our country, and with other multi-ethnic or multi-racial States in the Atlantic area. Thus similarities are revealed in the overall make-up of ethnic and other factors with those in Brazil, the cluster of Caribbean islands, Canada and the United States. Such is the case with the "American Indians" (from Latin America, Canada and the United States). Is it not a noble and achievable objective to revive the historical sociological links in order to provide a better future for the respective peoples? To paraphrase Susan GEORGE, "another world is possible"[136], as human genius has not ceased to demonstrate since the appearance of the first man on Earth – provided that alliances can be forged between peoples, or even better between States, for their development – provided that, a damper can be placed on those who believe in the coming of a messiah so that human beings can decide their own future. It is a Herculean task that has its roots in culture.

## B. THE CULTURAL DIMENSION

The concept of "culture", understood in a restrictive meaning, encompasses diverse elements, such as language, religion, law, science, the arts, customs and the skill to govern amongst others.

Culture also includes the scientific and intellectual advancement of a people and their society. Whether one understands "science with the aim of studying ideas, their laws, their nature, their link with the symbols that represent them and especially their origins"[137] as accepted by inventors, or in the belief that reproduces "as reality the expression of social information, particularly economic information, about which the person construing them is unaware, or at least does not realise that they shape his belief"[138]; ideology has its own part in culture.

In fact, culture is the sum total of man's activities. Two personalities as different as Cheik ANTA DIOP and Andrei GROMYKO are united

---

[136] GEORGE, S., *Un autre monde est possible si ...*, Paris, Fayard, 2004, 285 p.
[137] LALANDE, A., (ed.), *Vocabulaire technique et critique de la philosophie*, Paris, Presses universitaires de France, 1968, p. 458.
[138] *Ibid.* p. 459.

in their suggestions for a way out: "There is now nothing more that the vital elements in Africa can do than to get moving, and strengthen local culture and in so doing, develop the scientific and technological sectors"[139]. Saying that a strengthening of culture is needed is tantamount to admitting its existence.

It is appropriate to examine some of its major components.

## 1. Governance

With regard to one former important State in Congo, the comment of Diego CAO is worth quoting, "The Bakongo had achieved a developed level of culture"[140]. From where then did the cultural sub-development arise? Zala L. N'KANZA replied to the question of "whether the political power structure established in the Kongo before the Portuguese arrived (..) and then afterwards the Belgians, was a regime which was working towards the development of the Kongo inhabitants or more towards stagnation or political underdevelopment"[141]. Without beating around the bush, he declared that "on the whole, the political regime of the Kongo communities (...) was striving towards political development for the inhabitants of this country"[142]. Hence "it was more or less satisfying the need for participation, control, and the autonomy of decisions regarding the country's government"[143].

On the other hand, "if the political change which occurred in the Kongo must be judged and qualitatively compared" after the Portuguese occupation, "we shall say that there was some progression towards under-development"[144]. Even the elite were forced to "administer their communities in accordance with foreign values and standards"[145]. "Therefore, they could no longer be viewed by their population as highly revered spiritual leaders and symbols of irrefutable significance."[146].

---

[139] Cheikh ANTA DIOP, *op. cit.,* see also GROMYKO, A., *op. cit.* p. 257.
[140] KAKE, I. *et al., Conflit belgo-zaîrois, op. cit.,* p. 42
[141] N'KANZA, L., *op. cit.,* p. 84.
[142] *Ibid.,* p. 44.
[143] *Ibid.*
[144] *Ibid.,* p. 131.
[145] *Ibid.*
[146] *Ibid.*

There can be no challenging this sentence because it applies to all the colonial occupations that were inflicted upon Congo, "For more than three-quarters of a century, the Belgian colonial system excluded the entire African population living in the Belgian Congo from taking part in the political decision-making process or in controlling these decisions."[147]. Collette BRAECKMAN goes even further; the Congolese have been "dispossessed of the management of their own affairs for a century"[148], to such an extent that in 2009 she envisaged a "second independence for the Congo"[149].

After the Cold War, the notion of good governance became much clearer to the point that it has been almost universally recognised. In effect, it encompasses notions of democracy, alternating power, good management of municipal affairs, transparent management, respect of human rights and environmental protection.

Nowadays, good governance has become a measure of a State's standing and right to be heard in the international arena.

## 2. Language

With regard to linguistics, DRC has recognised four major languages, namely, Kikongo, Lingala, Kiswahili and Tshiluba. Most of these languages are also commonly used in other African countries. This is the case with Kikongo in Angola and Congo Brazzaville, Tshiluba in Angola, Lingala in Congo Brazzaville and in the Central African Republic and Kiswahili in Uganda, Rwanda, Burundi, Tanzania, Kenya and Zambia.

When considering the continent as a whole, Cheikh Anta DIOP's prophesy seems to be becoming true, "Kiswahili, a Bantu language from East Africa, has most chance of becoming the future language of government and culture for a unified Black Africa."[150] If "its vocabulary, like that of all the languages in the world, has been enormously enriched by outside influences (...), its grammar, i.e. its morphology

---

[147]  *Ibid.*, p. 15. This is also the opinion of C. BRAECKMAN, *Les nouveaux prédateurs...*, *op. cit.*, p. 107.
[148]  *Ibid.*
[149]  BRAECKMAN, C., *Vers la seconde indépendance du Congo*, *op. cit.*, p. 267.
[150]  DIOP, C. A., *op. cit.*, p. 112.

and syntax owe absolutely nothing to Arab, nor to any other foreign language", asserts the author[151].

It has to be admitted that in the aftermath of decolonisation "In East Africa for the first time, Black Africans dared to identify themselves by their own truly national culture"[152]. Since then, the African Union Parliament has made Kiswahili one of the working, though not official, languages. Maybe, tomorrow it will be adopted by the UN. According to sources quoted by the author, Kiswahili "is one of the twelve languages most widely spoken in the world"[153]. One of the main advantages of this language is that "its future expansion towards other populations does not involve any problem with cultural imperialism, from the small Waswahili nation for which this is their mother tongue", as this historian comments further. Though, as he points out, "this language is becoming more and more detached from the group of people speaking it at the outset, to become progressively part of the African cultural heritage"[154].

However, it is not intended to deride the cultural diversity that characterises DRC. The use of four national languages, namely Kikongo, Lingala, Kiswahili and Tshiluba, in the geographical areas indicated and even in the capital, are examples of this. These four languages also help to strengthen national identity. They play their part in the cultural unity within this diversity, sometimes alternatively, but in step with history.

Notwithstanding this diversity of languages, it cannot be denied that the Congolese, in an outpouring of pride and with patriotic fervour, share a strong feeling of belonging to one and the same nation. This feeling, called "nationalism" has been forged over a long period, in good and difficult times. It has been embodied in several speeches, deeds and gestures by successive leaders that the country has known. It emerges from what is conveniently known today as nationalist ideology or Congolese nationalism that the majority of leaders such as Lumumba, Mobutu, with his authentic Zairian nationalism, and M'zee Laurent-

---

[151]  *Ibid.*
[152]  *Ibid.*
[153]  *Ibid.*, p. 112.
[154]  *Ibid.*, p. 113.

Désiré Kabila who follows the same straight line as Lumumba, claimed to pursue.

## 3. Nationalism

Prior to DRC's constitution in its present form, nationalism charac-terised the resistance of the freedom movements which were intending to subdue firstly the Portuguese invaders and then those from Belgium.

Going back to origins permits false perceptions to be repudiated and according to which "as a political idea, nationalism is a recent phenomenon in DRC. No public or explicit demand for independence was observed by the Congolese leaders until 1956"[155]. It is one matter not to find, even not to want to notice a demand as natural as "the right to legitimate defence inbred in human nature"[156], including the human grouping collectively called the "State"; it is another to find the estab-lished presence of national feeling. For in the end, could populations who have lived freely, either in States, as Europe understands this insti-tution, or in independent groupings different from European structures that any moral, political, philosophical, economic, sociological, legal or other standard would create as a universal model, allow themselves to be subservient to any conqueror? Besides, what human science would expect nationalism to spout merely from the mouth of a leader?

The Algerian nationalist, anti-colonialist insurrection (1954-1962), unlike that in Indo-China, did not have any heroes. In the final analysis, people are the real heroes in these situations.

### a. Nationalism under Portuguese colonial occupation

In the guise of religion between the 16th and 17th centuries, a man named Kasola Francisco (1628-1634), a woman with the name of Mafuta and especially the famous Kimpa Vita (1684-1706) were standard-bearers for insurrection in the Kongo kingdom. Kasola was considered as "the saviour and liberator of the black race"[157]. He stamped a political and Pan-African mark on his movement. Because of his exploits, the

---

[155] YOUNG, C., *Introduction à la politique congolaise,* Kinshasa, Kisangani, Lubum-bashi, Brussels, CRISP, 1968, p. 138.
[156] AMMOUN, F., *op. cit.,* p. 69.
[157] NKANZA, L., *op. cit.,* p. 819.

people demanded "the expulsion of all missionaries from the Kongo"[158]. As for Mafuta, she had both a political and a religious role, encouraging King Kongo to "join together with the popular forces who were sympathetic towards him"[159].

However, the "Oscar" for Kongo nationalism in the 18th century belongs to the illustrious Kimpa Vita. In the wake of Kasola and Mafuta, she became head of the "National Liberation Movement"[160]. It was reported that this woman "popular with all levels of Kongolese society (...) saw her national liberation movement extend to all corners of the country due to the numerous disciples sent (...) to preach her message of national reunification"[161]. Condemned by an "ecclesiastical tribunal in Luwanda" not only under the pretext of having had "a son though unmarried"[162], but also and especially because of her subversive activities, she was burned alive, an *"autodafé* punishment inflicted upon heretics during the Middle Ages by the Roman Catholic Church"[163]. After this form of torture, "the Kongolese people were enraged"[164]. Kimpa Vita, baptised Dona Beatrice, was "the symbol of resistance in the kingdom towards the invader, embodying all things most noble and pure"[165]. There may have been other heroes and heroines who have fallen into oblivion.

All in all, a variety of nationalist movements have been present in the Independent State of Congo, the Belgian Congo and the independent Congo.

### b. *Nationalism under Belgian colonial occupation*

By means of an appropriate triptych "Early Independence Struggles", three authors inform us of many relevant events. It is interesting to focus upon them. Even before 1939, some Congolese groups had begun to campaign for emancipation, although such terms as "autono-

---

[158]   *Ibid.*
[159]   *Ibid.*, p. 120.
[160]   *Ibid.*
[161]   *Ibid.*, p. 121.
[162]   *Ibid.*
[163]   *Ibid.*
[164]   *Ibid.*
[165]   *Ibid.*

mous government" or "Independence" were still rare[166]. This is exactly the moment when Belgian colonisation began in earnest. Hence, the authors reject the imprecise statement by Crawford Young mentioned above. Similar movements were violent, these were:

1. the Mbole resistance, beginning in 1908;
2. the Upper-Uélé insurrection, from 1915 to 1917;
3. insurrections in Lomami, Sankuru, Equator and Lake Leopold II, from 1919 to 1921[167];
4. the Kivu insurrection, from 1921 to 1923;
5. the Kwango insurrection, from 1930 to 1931[168].

Despite this, none of these revolts was able to obtain much wider support[169]. If they lacked the political figures likely to unite them, the revolts did nevertheless express nationalist resistance against Belgian colonial oppression. Yet, the names of heroes became known during these anti-colonial insurrections. One in particular was Bwana-Kienda who, in 1917, led the uprising against the settlers laying the rail-line to link Kalule-North with Katanga. The settlers skinned him alive in the Drooplans Square in Elisabethville (Lubumbashi)[170].

Furthermore, one of the important movements was the campaign of the millennium led by Simon Kimbangu. The movement developed even more quickly than its leader. Soldiers and urban officials left their jobs to join Kimbangu's movement. This movement gave rise to a series of reports and legendary accounts in all parts of the country[171]

Even after its leader was captured, the movement continued in secrecy. At the end of the 1930s, Simon-Pierre Mpadi organised a revival of the Kimbangu movement before the Belgians forced him into exile[172].

---

[166]  RENTON, D., et al., op. cit., p. 63.
[167]  Ibid.
[168]  Ibid., p. 64.
[169]  Ibid.
[170]  Ibid.
[171]  Ibid. KAKE, I. et al., op. cit., p. 48, describe him as a nationalist from the outset. Arrested in 1921 and condemned for disturbance of the peace, he died "in prison after 30 years' detention", like no other known African leader.
[172]  RENTON, D. et al., op. cit., p. 65.

Even if Kimbangu, as a ploy, had insisted on the apolitical nature of his movement, it was not possible to ignore the significance of this mass movement emanating from Africans and lead totally by Congolese[173]. The colonial authorities did not make any mistake in their interpretation of the political movement whose particular demand was that natives should no longer work for Europeans, or pay tax to the government[174]. Plainly, this was an appeal for a political boycott addressed to all Congolese people.

It is also useful to mention briefly the uprisings of the workers in Katanga from 1941; their aim was to take part in the job of dismantling the colonial regime and creating a sovereign Congolese nation. From November 1914, the miners of Jadotville, Kipushi, Likasi, Luisha and the metalworkers of Elisabethville began to plan a type of general strike. During the night of 3 December 1941, the workers at Shituru and Pandotville voted for a general strike on the following day. Strikers were dispatched to areas close to Likasi, Luishia and Kambove to seek support. This regional strike depended upon an alliance between factory workers in Elisabethville and Jadotville together with miners from Kipushi. Along with the workers, wives and mothers played a decisive role[175]. The strike spread and, on 9 December, workers from all Union Miniere's sites had rallied together[176]. This strike led to a change in working conditions in the mines and an awakening of the Congolese workers' awareness[177].

Between February and May 1944, there was an attempted military "insurrection" in Katanga. Planned to involve the entire Congo, the revolt was defeated by a series of preventative arrests. After conquering the town of Luluabourg, the rebels were then forced to beat a retreat. The Kolwezi and Luishia miners were allies of the soldiers and helped them escape to safety in Angola. They also had help and support from peasants in Kasai and Katanga. The strike on the Matadi docks in 1945 is another noteworthy event[178]. To say "the Belgians, in complete good

---

[173]  *Ibid.*
[174]  *Ibid.*
[175]  *Ibid.*, p. 67.
[176]  *Ibid.*, p. 68.
[177]  *Ibid.*, p. 69.
[178]  *Ibid.*, p. 70.

faith, saw nothing coming" [179] seems to err on the side of over-simplification, if not total ignorance. Some colonial leaders were indeed aware of the dramatic evolution of the situation. It was in fact a decade before the declarations by the civil and religious, African colonial administrators in Leopoldville. Not only would it be impossible to study nationalism through legal or other formal avenues, but the abovementioned social events convey more expressively and illustrate more clearly the waves of protest against colonial power.

With regard to the Kivu uprising, from 1921 to 1923, the studies of Professor NJANGU CANDA CIRI demonstrate that the colonial occupation in the East of the country did not happen without fierce resistance from leaders of the tribes and local kingdoms who took action on several occasions to protect their subjects and their land from the invaders. Some lost their life in so doing and others were quite simply exiled. The colonial power unsuccessfully tried several times to weaken and subdue the traditional leaders. The author would in this connection mention the exile to Leopoldville of the Chief of the Bashi, Mwami Alexandre Kabare, in 1921, and before him, that of Chief Nyalukemba to Fizi, etc. [180]

Not only was Congolese nationalism not born yesterday but it is still shaping the prevalent ideology of the entire Congolese people, evident since independence, although it has lately suffered some erosion.

Four reasons [181] may be given for the delayed expression of Congolese nationalism, which are namely: the lack of qualified leaders, the prohibition of political parties, the absence of a free press, and the compulsory framework, i.e. the legal system, established for a colonised population. Though the political and social situation on which this nationalism depends does not depend upon any series of decrees.

---

[179]  BRAECKMAN, C., *Vers la deuxième indépendance...op. cit.*, p. 18.
[180]  NJANGU, C., "Notes sur les sources orales de la première résistance shi", *Etud. Biet. Ff* (Lubumbashi), 7, 1975, pp. 203-206. And by the same author, "La résistance shi à la pénetration européenne (1900-1920)", degree dissertation, Université nationale du Zaïre, Lubumbashi campus, 1974.
[181]  YOUNG, Cr., *op. cit.*, pp. 141-142.

## c. Nationalism under neo-colonial authority

Neocolonialism, except when the State apparatus is massively in the hands of foreign "experts" or international "consultants", produces a false image of the situation in the country occupied. This is why this last term is not often used, even though the debate is still on-going. The Sovereign National Conference (1991-1992) found the right words to describe the decolonisation of the Congo as "independence deliberately rushed through by Belgium"[182].

The facts are well known. After the victory of the nationalist faction led by Patrice Lumumba[183] in the general election organised in 1960 by the Belgian colonial power, which, unpleasantly surprised by the prospective emancipation of its only colony, started to foster anarchy in Congo. It carried out various illicit acts. On 4 July 1960, General Janssens, in command of the colonial army, wrote on a blackboard on the parade ground of the main barracks in the city of Leopoldville (Kinshasa) that the situation "after independence is the same as before independence". Then a mutiny started in the "Police force"[184]. Belgium used this as a pretext to deploy its paratroopers in Congo, in 1960, to protect its compatriots from danger[185].

The alleged state of necessity claimed by Belgium induced several eminent jurists such as Arechaga and Tanzi, to assert that there was no reason to talk of a state of necessity[186], especially when this kind of conduct could be in breach of a compulsory norm. At Belgium's instigation, "Katanga declared its secession on 11 July 1960 and South-Kasai ... on 8 August 1960"[187].

The UN, dominated in the main and especially in the Security Council by the Western States, did not condemn the Belgian armed aggression notwithstanding the fact that from 10 to 18 July 1960,

---

[182]  BULA-BULA, S., *op. cit.*, p. 104 whilst YOUNG, Cr., *op. cit.*, p. 171 describes it as "the most disorganised decolonisation in all Africa".
[183]  BULA-BULA, S., *op. cit.*, p. 103.
[184]  *Ibid.*
[185]  HENKIN, L., PUGH, R. C., SCHACHTER, O., SMIT, H., *International Law. Cases and Materials,* 3rd Edition, West Publishing Company, St. Paul, Minn., 1993, p. 565.
[186]  *Ibid.*
[187]  BULA-BULA, S., *op. cit.*, p. 103.

"Belgian troops intervened in 28 towns"[188]. Additionally, "in Matadi, the Belgian navy, for no reason, bombed the town that the Whites had already completely evacuated"[189]. In its resolution on 14 July 1960, the Security Council restricted itself to inviting Belgium to withdraw its troops from Congo[190].

## C. ABORTIVE ATTEMPS TO DISMEMBER CONGO

With unwavering determination, Belgium provoked the secession of Katanga, the province considered to be the richest in Congo. The secession of South-Kasai was proclaimed on 8 August 1960, also at Belgium's instigation. To further the secession, "Belgian troops were used to disarm and repel all Congolese troops, who did not come from the pro-CONAKAT areas of the province"[191]. Clearly, "Belgian intervention (...) was assisting the secession of Katanga"[192].

It was exactly the same with the South-Kasai secession to control the diamond industry.

But Congolese nationalism which existed in the period prior to the arrival of the Whites caused the failure of these attempts to carve up the country.

### 1. Decapitation of government and emergence of nationalist movements

The culmination of Belgian colonialist manoeuvres occurred when the country was implicated in the assassination of Prime Minister Lumumba, in January 1961, that of the Senate's Vice President, Joseph Okito, and the Minister for Youth, Maurice Mpolo. Never again did the

---

[188]  YOUNG, Cr., *op. cit.*, p. 169.

[189]  *Ibid.*, p. 168.

[190]  VERHAEGEN, B., *Rébellions au Congo*, volume 1, Brussels, CRISP, Leopoldville, IRES, INEP, 1966, pp. 32-33, criticizes "the action of the UN forces in the Congo". Sometimes the UN "protected the leaders on the spot" sometimes its "intervention (...) was openly against specific leaders (...) on behalf of the adversaries; this was the case when Lumumba's government fell in August-September 1960, with the Gizenga regime in Stanleyville (Kisangani) in January 1962 and the Tschombe government in Katanga in January 1963."

[191]  YOUNG, Cr., *op. cit.*, p. 169.

[192]  *Ibid.*

Congo experience true rule of order, nor real peace on its entire territory[193].

The Leopoldville authorities, illegal in the eyes of the majority of the Congolese electorate, thereafter had to face up to a popular ground swell that threatened to wash them away.

The sovereign National Conference, in 1992, decided to "open proceedings". It proposed that the "assassinations of Lumumba, Mpolo and Okito, although they were not classed in the categories currently defined by the United Nations, should be considered as crimes against humanity for they involved persecution and assassinations for political reasons"[194]. Previously, a historical hurricane had been unleashed when the assassination of Lumumba was announced at the beginning of 1961.

Lumumba's death made him a historical figure, worshiped by all the progressive factions of the era.

Displaying the limits of her knowledge of Black Africa, Catherine COQUERY-VIDROVITCH called the first, popular, revolutionary insurrections experienced by Congo in decolonised Africa "the largest peasants' revolt of the century"[195]. More to the point, Benoit VERHAEGEN, who had conducted on the spot research, justifiably described it as the "first significant revolutionary insurrection in Africa"[196].

What is more, in the twilight of his life, he corrected the confused description of the Kwilu rebellion that this former officer from the Belgian battalion in Korea[197] had made on one of the major events characterising nationalist resistance to the nascent neo-colonialism in Congo. Previously, he had objectively recognised that "the cultural divide between the researcher (European) and the subject of his

---

[193]  YOUNG, Cr., *op. cit.*, p. 171 and ss.

[194]  BULA-BULA, S. *op. cit.* p. 104.

[195]  COQUERY-VIDROVITCH, C., *op. cit.*, p. 229.

[196]  VERHAEGEN, B., *op. cit.*, p. 33.

[197]  VERHAEGEN, B. served in the Belgian battalion amongst the western allies in the war between capitalism and communism in Korea. His impartial opinion on the tragic events in the Congo, which, according to unfortunate timing, occurred during the Cold War is therefore to be considered with caution. Nevertheless, three years before he died, he was able to rectify his analysis in the mid-1960s. See VERHAEGEN, B., OMASOMBO, J., SIMONS, E., VERHAEGEN, F., *Mulele et la revolution populaire au Kwilu (République démocratique du Congo)*, Cahiers africains – Africa studies, n° 72, 2006, Paris, L'Harmattan, 2006, 364 p.

research (African society) was not conducive to facilitate any awareness and interpretation of social phenomena and their outcome"[198].

Lumumba's assassination and the attempts to carve up Congo caused various movements to call themselves nationalist; some were political, some military, or were both at the same time.

## 2. Nationalist resistance erupts into violence over three-quarters of Congo

Four rebellions, with underlying nationalist ideology, tried to ensure continuity of Patrice Emery Lumumba's ideology in the wake of the brutal overthrow of his government. These were the following rebellions: in Kwilu, starting in 1963, North-Katanga in 1964, the Eastern province and also in the region of Uvira and Fizi-baraka in 1964.

All these rebellions could not put an end to the Mobutu regime, which had the support of the Western Bloc during the Cold War period. It was not until 17 May 1997 that the Congolese nationalist wing, led by Laurent-Désiré Kabila, came back to Kinshasa, helped by political and military support from Rwanda, Burundi and Uganda.

This revolution in May 1997 drove a sick Mobutu from power in Zaire, today known as the Democratic Republic of Congo, after so many years during which the regime had been weakened by political parties created after liberalisation in the political sphere under the leadership and aura of Etienne Tshisekedi wa Mulumba and his companions. This was also in essence a revolution but by peaceful means which, although it did not exactly put an end to Mobutu's dictatorship, it did wear it away sufficiently to further the revolutionary aims of an alliance of democratic liberation forces in Congo, led by Laurent-Désiré Kabila.

From the foregoing, we think that it is wrong to consider the resistance movements led by men, victims of unconstitutional changes, as being rebellious. For disobedience to established law and order, on 30 June 1960, was a result of the behaviour of politicians who had benefited from their connection with the forces of the day. These politicians were in fact in the pocket of the colonial power which, constrained by events, had precipitated independence with the intention of recouping the situation later.

---

[198]  *Ibid.*, p. 15.

Above and beyond considerations linked to Congolese nationalism, briefly outlined above, it is to be noted that globalisation is the order of the day. Economies no longer recognise national frontiers. Questions may be raised as to the influence of ideologies on the progress and development of nations now, at the beginning of the 21$^{st}$ century.

Far from misjudging their significance, the era of ideologies unravelling like a string of ideas and thoughts conceived as a base and stimulation for the development of man and society seems to have gone out of fashion in favour of an era with a general and mutually advantageous cooperation, the transfer of technology, in short the work of nations. This explains the weakening, if not the disappearance of the East-West Blocs.

Hence, it may be asserted that independently of a few temporary flare-ups and friction between some of DRC's tribes, the country has sufficient resources to exploit the wealth which nature has so generously bestowed upon it.

# Partial conclusion – Part One

Nobody can now deny the important role played by DRC during the last five centuries. This role is due to both its geographical and geostrategic position at the heart of the African Continent and also the exploitation of the socio-cultural situation (the importance of human and cultural resources) and the economic situation (the importance of natural resources: mining, forestry and agricultural) which have enabled the country to assert its position in international relations.

Such advantages and opportunities should have enabled the country to achieve economic and social development for the benefit of its citizens.

# DRC: ECONOMIC POTENTIAL CONTRASTED WITH LEVEL OF DEVELOPMENT AND REALISTIC EXPECTATIONS

# Introduction

It is no exaggeration to describe DRC's subsoil as a truly geological disgrace. However, it is not possible to prevent the distinction being made between its enormous potential and the level of the current development of the country. It has suffered substantially from the effects of economic, financial and food crises through the fault of its leaders who were not able to protect it from bad government but led it to the edge of the abyss. The country is in crisis and finds it difficult to overcome the situation in spite of efforts made by public authorities for over a decade.

Faced with the world crisis, men become increasingly aware of the precarious nature of their destiny and are forced to seek solutions.

This means that a country must change its current course and create conditions to revitalise the economy. Of course, those especially blessed with mining, agricultural and other natural resources should be able to reach a position where they are prepared for any challenges which may arise.

How have the Congolese reacted to this fight for survival in the economic and social crisis over time and how do they expect to find lasting solutions?

If the stagnation into which the country has been plunged is due to many and varied reasons, it would seem useful to explain the economic and social dimensions of the current crisis (Chapter I) and the diplomatic and security aspects aimed to stabilise the situation (Chapter II).

# CHAPTER I

# Economic and social dimensions of the crisis

The economic and social dimensions of the crisis allow a better understanding of the disparity and imbalance existing between on one hand, the potential resources which are exploited and managed improvidently and on the other hand, the level of development achieved.

## I. Economic dimension [199]

The Congolese economy has been made captive by the programme marked out by the coloniser, the backbone of which was the transport system. It is fundamentally oriented towards what is to be extracted and then exported.

Extraction, because it was and remains based on the production of mineral and agricultural raw materials, without any structure for local reprocessing.

Exportation, because the raw materials produced were to be exported to Belgium for processing purposes.

At independence, DRC had achieved the same level of development as Canada, Korea, Brazil and South Africa.

With a population of 14.65 million, it had a Gross Domestic Product of 522.36 USD per person, which is an income of a little more than 360 USD per capita per year. This figure was only 180 USD in 2008.

Its currency had the same value as that of Belgium, with a parity of one Congolese franc equal to one Belgian franc. In recent times, the Congolese franc has been fluctuating quite a lot in comparison with

---

[199] See TAMBWE KITENGE, E., MAKOSSO COLLINET, A. (ed.), *RDCongo: les élections et après ? Intellectuels et politiques posent les enjeux de l'après-transition*, Paris, l'Harmattan, Géo-écostrapol, 2006; Banque centrale du Congo, Annual reports 2002-2003, 2003-2004, 2004-2005, 2005-2006 and 2006-2007; République démocratique du Congo, Programme minimum de partenariat pour la transition et la relance (PMPTR) en République démocratique du Congo, November 2004.

foreign currency; when going to print, it was around 1000 Congolese franc to one dollar.

In his analysis of the evolution of the economic and social situation of DRC from independence until 1997, Professor Evariste MABI MULUMBA commented that "the total size of the economy reverted to the 1958 level whilst its population had tripled in the meantime, increasing from 15 million citizens in 1958 to the current 45 million"[200].

The country's economy was sustained by the production of copper and cobalt (GECAMINES, ex-Union Miniere of Upper-Katanga), diamonds (MIBA, Miniere de Bakwanga), gold (Office des Mines d'Or de Kilo-Moto), coffee, palm oil, cotton, rubber, tea, etc.

This production makes DRC the number one cobalt, industrial diamond, and palm oil worldwide producer and the fifth worldwide copper producer.

But with the oil crisis in 1971 which caused the drop in metal prices on the international market, together with the untimely steps towards "Zairianisation" (nationalisation) of plantations and other production centres in 1973, DRC's economy suffered a crash which was made worse by successive wars and rebellions.

Whilst it had achieved an annual production of 475 to 500,000 tons of copper and 12,000 tons of cobalt during the 1980s, DRC currently only produces 20,000 tons of copper and 3,000 tons of cobalt per year.

The grandiose policy of the Second Republic, dominated by expenditure on prestigious projects (construction of "white elephants") and the party-State, neglected investments and renovation of the means for production.

Consequence: the production capacity collapsed and the country exports very little agricultural products. Not a single litre of palm oil is exported. As for exports, in the main they comprise just wood, coffee, tea, diamonds and handicrafts.

---

[200] MABI MULUMBA, E., *Les dérives d'une gestion prédatrice*, Kinshasa, Centre de Recherches pédagogiques, 1998.

This situation has had a disastrous effect on the currency, and with a lack of export income, budgets are not sufficient for either the country's size or its population.

The basic infrastructure (roads, rail, public building), social (schools and hospitals) and scientific infrastructure (universities and research centres) are undergoing a consequent and indescribable deterioration.

Moreover, the constraints on structural improvements imposed by international financial institutions, particularly the World Bank, the International Monetary Fund, the African Development Bank, in conjunction with the generalised corruption, has not allowed the country to achieve the results anticipated. Cooperation, sometimes started then interrupted for failing to respect performance criteria, is additionally perceived by national opinion as a bad policy given the budgetary restraints (reductions in costs and salaries as well as a reduced number of personnel in public service).

And yet, the non-compliance with the terms and conditions imposed by the international donor organisations is due mainly to bad governance: lack of transparency in the management of public funds, obstacles to parliamentary control, political favouritism, generalised corruption, unjustifiable accumulation of wealth, tax and customs fraud, malfunctioning of the legal system, all of which create a bad business environment.

For several years the country has been rushing to achieve the target of the HIPC initiative, in order to claim a sizeable reduction in its external debt which amounts to approximately 14 billion US dollars. In 2010, a decision was made to alleviate this by some 90 %. In spite of this, the question is whether from now on the country can benefit from a sum of money made available to its leaders even though they were unable to perform any better with the "mountain" of money already received.

Yet the country has great potential which is only waiting to be exploited to improve the economic and social environment.

In order to better manage the resources concerned, specific legislation has been adopted. (Mining Code, Forestry Code) or is being drafted (Hydrocarbon Code, Agricultural Code, Code for Water), based upon the Code on Investments.

However, the application of these laws causes various problems such as doubts about the commitments already made. Hence the revision of mining contracts often seems like legal insecurity in the minds of external investors. This government practice of constantly going back on commitments made does not give it any credibility with external partners. Likewise, the demand for commission payments by the authorities concerned with the creation of enterprises, usually with foreign capital, damages the country's reputation and causes it to lose a great deal of investment.

DRC must endeavour to negotiate the most appropriate mining agreements once and for all in order to reassure its partners. Investors should not have to pay for the mistakes of the Administration nor the lack of attention to detail from managers entrusted with negotiations.

Whatever the outcome, DRC's potential is still intact in the mining, oil or agricultural sectors.

Steps to be taken in these fields should tend towards the identification of and guarantees on resources and, in compliance with the law, the negotiation of exploitation contracts with partners on a "win-win" basis, to foster local reprocessing industries.

Reviving the production of the country's entire resources will have a definite positive impact on the economy and the infrastructure (roads, schools, hospitals, research centres, etc.).

Before any presentation of the opportunities available, it is appropriate just to welcome potential partners and say something about bilateral and multilateral cooperation in the economic field.

## A. ECONOMIC TIES WITH BRETTON WOODS INSTITUTIONS AND SOME ATLANTIC STATES

For several years DRC has been a member of the international financial institutions (World Bank, International Monetary Fund and the African Development Bank) and also the World Trade Organisation. It trades with countries bordering the Atlantic from the North to the South. They include European Union countries (Germany, Belgium, Spain, France, Italy, Portugal, the United Kingdom, etc.), the United States, Canada, Brazil, South Africa, Angola, Nigeria, Morocco, etc.

## 1. Cooperation with Bretton Woods institutions

Regarding relationships with Bretton Woods[201] institutions, cooperation with these bodies, though interrupted in 1990, was revived after nearly a decade due to the creation of several programmes: the *Programme Intérimaire Renforcé* (PIR) (DRC's Provisional Reinforced Programme), the *Programme Multisectoriel d'Urgence et Reconstruction et de Réhabilitation* (PMURR) (the Emergency Reconstruction and Rehabilitation Multi-sector Programme), and the *Programme Minimum de Partenariat pour la Transition et la Relance* (PMPTR) (Partnership for Transition and Revival Minimum Programme)[202].

The revival of this cooperation materialised with the first *Programme Économique du Gouvernement* (PEG$_1$) (Government Economic Programme), which was agreed with the IMF in April 2002 under the title of the *Facilité pour la Réduction de la Pauvreté et pour la Croissance* (FRPC) (the Poverty Reduction and Growth Facility – PRGF). Non-compliance with the commitments made by the Transitional Government (1 + 4), following unanticipated expenditure during the last three months of 2005 and the first three months of 2006, led the IMF to formally withdraw from the PEG$_1$ on 31 March 2006.

Following intensive negotiations, a second government economic programme PEG$_2$ was agreed on 11 December 2009 between the IMF and DRC, for three years, backdated from 1 July 2009 until 3 June 2012. The PEG$_2$ also depends upon the PRGF (the Poverty Reduction and Growth Facility) and involves 346.45 million SDR (Special Drawing Rights) (approximately 551.45 million USD).

The IMF Executive Board also approved a provisional additional aid of 45.66 million SDR (approximately 72.68 million USD) under the Heavily Indebted Poor Countries (HIPC) reinforced initiative, in order to reduce DRC's repayment to service its debt with the IMF. The anticipated payment of funds, some 78.5 million USD per period, is conditional upon the results at the end of each of six reviews[203].

---

[201] The United States of America and the European Union countries are the main contributors to the IMF, with 16.79% and 32,1% of voting rights, respectively. They also exert great influence within the World Bank.

[202] See DRC, PMPTR, Kinshasa, November 2004.

[203] Cf. *Le Potentiel* n° 4803 of 14 December 2009, p. 2.

The objective of the PEG$_2$ is to permit DRC to fulfil the conditions of the HIPC initiative and substantially reduce its external debt. End-2008, the OGEDEP (*Office de Gestion de la Dette Publique*, or Public debt management office) limited the amount of public debt to 12.042 billion dollars, 10.753 billion of which was for the external debt. This is 55.5% owed to the Paris Club (United States, France, Japan, Italy, Belgium, Germany, the Netherlands, Canada, etc.), 39.3% to multilateral organisations (World Bank, IMF, AfDB, etc.), 4.7% to the Kinshasa Club and 0.3% to the London Club[204].

The PEG$_2$'s programme of structural reforms also has the objective of ensuring a further increase in revenue, to improve the management and quality of public expenditure, to strengthen the financial system, particularly by restructuring the Central Bank, and to improve the business climate[205].

The macroeconomic plan should obtain the following results: an annual average increase in the real GDP of 5.5%, a 9% rate of inflation at the end of the period, gross reserves equivalent to ten weeks' imports, not including aid, from now until 2012, as well as a limitation of the current external deficit (including aid) to an average 25% of GDP[206].

The agreement on the PEG$_2$ was the result of several meetings between the Congolese government and IMF leaders, but also with countries holding important voting rights within the IMF, Paris Club Members and countries around the Atlantic (United States, Canada, Belgium, France, the Netherlands, etc.).

It is, however, necessary to mention the successive failures of different programmes with the International Monetary Fund since President Mobutu's era.

In effect, the fundamental architecture of all the restructuring policies advocated by the International Monetary Fund relied upon the "development strategy of the Washington Consensus"[207]. This strategy is oriented towards the following objectives: "to reduce the role of the

---

[204]  Cf. *Le Potentiel* n° 4756 of 20 October 2009, p. 9.
[205]  Cf. *Le Potentiel* n° 4803 of 14 December 2009, p. 2.
[206]  *Ibid.*
[207]  STIGLITZ, J., *Un autre Monde, contre le fanatisme du marché*, Paris, Fayard, 2006, p. 61.

State to the absolute minimum and favour privatisation (...), freedom of trade and access to capital markets (...) and also deregulation (the suppression of rules imposed on companies)"[208].

It is apparent that these policies, which have not been successful, even in countries with a basic infrastructure and a minimum of organisation in public institutions, have not had any positive impact to-date in DRC.

## 2. Cooperation with Atlantic States

The Atlantic is a commercial trade area not just for the countries bordering it but also between these and the rest of the world. International trade is currently governed by the World Trade Organisation (WTO)[209]; which succeeded the General Agreement on Tariffs and Trade (GATT).

The norms which were agreed at the Uruguay Round and GATT in 1994[210] apply to DRC in its trade with countries bordering the Atlantic, in particular the non-discrimination principle, and the rules on protection by customs duties and the general elimination of quantitative restrictions on volumes.

### a. European Union Member States

On the basis of GATT article XXIV, the countries in the Group of African, Caribbean and Pacific States (ACP), of which DRC is a member, finalised cooperation agreements with the European Union. This partnership is currently governed by the Cotonou Agreement, revised in Luxemburg on 25 June 2005. The ACP-EU trade relationship departs from some of the GATT principles on non-discrimination and the application of the clause on most favoured nation status, in which the European market accepts a franchise system for basic products from ACP countries, without any requirement for reciprocal arrangements.

---

[208] *Ibid.*, p. 61.
[209] For an analysis of this matter, see BAKANDEJA wa MPUNGU, G., *Le droit du commerce international. Les peurs justifiées de l'Afrique face à la mondialisation des marchés*, Kinshasa/Brussels, Afrique Editions – De Boeck & Larcier, 2001; LUFF, D., *Le droit de l'Organisation Mondiale du Commerce. Analyse critique*, Brussels/Paris, Bruylant – LGDJ, 2004.
[210] See GATT, *The results of the Uruguay Round of multilateral trade negotiations. Legal texts, Geneva 1994*

Aiming to create free trade zones, a new strategy saw the light of day in the form of the Economic Partnership Agreement (EPA) between the European Union and the six ACP regions. This strategy might be criticised as a means to get round global mechanisms. Several issues have been singled out: access of goods to markets, the trade in services, assistance to trade, the fixing and definition of net tax implications, etc.

To clarify the situation on the EPA negotiations between the European Union and Central Africa, DRC's former Minister for the Economy and Trade, the much missed André-Philippe Futa, identified areas of divergence with European Union partners, and in particular: the lack of a real strategy for regional integration, the rate of progress towards an open market, additional resources to be allocated to compensate for loss of customs revenue, the time limits for preparatory and transitional periods, the non-execution clause, application of the most favoured nation clause and the extension to the scope of the EPA[211].

Besides the bilateral and multilateral ties between the European Union and DRC[212], the latter has trade ties with European countries bordering the Atlantic (Belgium, Spain, France, Portugal, the United Kingdom, etc.). Congolese exports to the European Union mainly comprise the following products: pearls, precious stones and metals, coffee, tea, wood, and minerals. The main imports from the European Union are: vehicles, mechanical equipment and motors, milled flour products, meats and offal, pharmaceutical products, electrical equipment, publications, textiles, cereal-based goods, etc.[213]

DRC could improve its trade balance with the European Union if it would address some specific concerns, in particular: the competitiveness of goods for export, the processing of goods, compliance with norms, the improved trade capacity and simplification of export procedures.

---

[211] Speech at the opening ceremony of the awareness and information seminar for parliamentarians on the negotiations for the Economic Partnership Agreement (EPA), Kinshasa, 22 June 2009

[212] See MAVUNGU, J.-P., "Réflexion sur la coopération multisectorielle entre l'Union européenne et la RDC au regard des Conventions de Lomé et l'Accord de Cotonou", *Law Faculty Review*, n° 5, the Protestant University of the Congo, 2007, pp. 235-258.

[213] Cf. European Commission delegation, *Economic report by the European Commission delegation to the DRC*, 2000-2001, Kinshasa, September 2002, pp. 43-45.

## b. United States of America

In 2000, The United States of America adopted the law on growth and economic opportunities in Africa (the African Growth and Opportunity Act – AGOA) with the goal of not just opening up the American market to imports of African products, but also to develop stock markets in a variety of African countries.

In addition, commercial trade has tripled between 2000 and 2008, increasing from 29.3 to 104.6 billion USD, respectively. The United States are one of the three main trading partners on the continent, together with the European Union and China[214].

They import the following products from the African continent: oil (75.5%), minerals and metals (7.6%), vehicles and spare parts (2.2%), textiles and clothes (1.2%), cocoa (1%), etc. It should be mentioned that, because of the economic crisis, American imports within the framework of the AGOA decreased by 61% during the first five months of 2009[215].

The prospects for cooperation in the commercial arena really exist between the United States and DRC. The Americans are interested in oil and minerals (uranium, copper, cobalt, coltan, gold, manganese, bauxite, coal, methane gas, etc.). They could also help to improve agricultural production and profitability of energy resources in DRC[216]. In this respect, the project for maize production in North-Katanga (previously known as North-Shaba) that had worked well until the departure of the Americans can be suitably recalled.

Several American products flood the Congolese markets: vehicles, food products, textiles, electromechanical equipment and motors, etc. Just as in many African countries, (Ghana, Mauritius, Rwanda, Uganda and Kenya for example) DRC can improve its economic growth by means of the AGOA. To do this, the government and the economic players have to work in concert to conquer the American market, through a series of ambitious measures and initiatives: such as the diversification of products, an improvement in the quality of products, a reorganisation of marketing methods, compliance with delivery dates, exchanges of economic missions, etc.

---

[214]  Cf. Jeune Afrique, http://www.jeuneafrique.com.
[215]  *Ibid.*
[216]  Cf. *Le Potentiel* n° 4686 of 29 July 2009, p. 2.

## c. Canada

Canada is an important partner amongst the Atlantic countries. In its capacity as Co-President of the group of friends of the Great Lakes Region, Canada supports the work of the International Conference on the Region of the Great Lakes (ICRGL). This Conference is the principal international forum aiming to provide lasting solutions to problems of peace, security, stability and development in the Region.

The Canadian International Development Agency (CIDA) administers the bilateral development aid programme with DRC and also participates in numerous multilateral initiatives oriented towards peace, good governance, poverty reduction and humanitarian aid.

Although commercial trade between Canada and DRC is still very limited and in 2008, Canadian exports to the country were worth 38,142,051 USD whilst Canadian imports from DRC were worth 2,941,903 USD)[217]. Some Canadian companies have made considerable investment in DRC, to such an extent that Canada is considered the largest non-African investor in the country's mining sector.

Some of the most noticeable Canadian mining companies are as follows: Banro, Kinross-Forrest, Barrick Gold, Emaxon, Lundin (Tenke Fungurume Mining), Mindev, Anvil Mining, and First Quantum Minerals Ltd. Some of these are good examples to show the influence of Canadian mining companies in DRC. An exhaustive list would be too long and certainly too disparate.

Finally there ought to be a reaffirmation of the need to increase the scope of the bilateral and trade agreements between DRC and Canada, which are two countries with significant transatlantic aims and objectives[218].

## d. Brazil

As an emerging country and a G20 member, Brazil has ambitions to consolidate its position on the international scene and to gain access to new and promising markets, as an equal competitor with the traditional

---

[217] Sources: Statistique/industrie canada, http://strategis.ici.gd.ca, IMF: http://www.imf.org/external/data.htm, October 2009.

[218] For further information, cf. the Canadian government website: www.international.gc.ca.

players (the United States of America, France, Portugal, etc.) as with other emerging countries (China, India, and South Korea)[219]. Following decades of political upheaval and mixed growth, Brazil is now poised to occupy a prominent position in the world economy.

Commercial ties between the DRC and Brazil have experienced remarkable growth over the past few years. The volume of bilateral trade increased from 17 million USD in 2005 to 210 million in 2007, an increase of 1,235 %.

Several Brazilian companies are established in DRC, the most important of which are: Vale (active in the mining sector in Katanga), HRT-Petroleum (evaluation of oil reserves in the Central Congolese Basin), Commercial Transport Agency (importation of machines and equipment for the mining industry), and Adex Sprl (diamond trade), etc.

DRC imports various products from Brazil: notably poultry (33.6 %), cereals (21.5 %) sugar and confectionery products (14.8 %), cattle (5.4 %) and plastics (3.6 %)[220]. As for Congolese exports to Brazil, these are mainly mining products and oil[221].

In order to rekindle the multi-sector cooperation between Brazil and DRC, the latter can benefit from the Brazilian experience to change its status from an LDC and obtain that of an emerging country; especially since Brazilian technical cooperation is one of the priorities in the foreign policy of President Luiz Inacio Lula da Silva.

The strengthening of commercial ties with other countries in the region (Argentina, Mexico, Venezuela, etc) is also necessary to lengthen the list of our transatlantic partners.

## 3. Cooperation in Sub-Saharan Africa

DRC is located at the centre of Africa. This position, which enables it to belong to several sub-regional organisations, is an indication of the key role to be played in the economic growth of the constituent States, members of these organisations. Such organisations are: the Economic Community of Central African States (ECCAS), the Economic Community of the Great Lakes Countries (ECGLC), the Southern African

---

[219] Cf. MILANI, C., "Brésil, objectifs diplomatiques", *Courrier de la planète*, n° 84.
[220] *Ibid.*
[221] Cf. http://www.digitalcongo.net

Development Community (SADC) and also the Common Market for Eastern and Southern Africa (COMESA).

Membership of various regional organisations increases DRC's chances of commercial ties as well as economic, fiscal and legislative integration, which is likely to expand the opportunities for growth in the whole of Africa, starting with DRC. In this connection, the New Partnership for Africa's Development (NEPAD), which has a vision and strategic framework for the resurgence of Africa, considers DRC as pivotal in the development of the entire African continent.

## B. ECONOMIC OPPORTUNITIES IN DRC

The energy and mining situation, opportunities in the agricultural and livestock sectors and issues linked to the conservation and protection of the environment will be covered under the scope of this subject.

### 1. Energy situation

DRC is well endowed with fresh water and possesses enormous energy potential due to the existence of hydrocarbons and hydroelectric dams.

*a. Hydrocarbons*

Petroleum, bituminous shale and gas are the main hydrocarbons to be found in DRC.

As far as petroleum is concerned, the country has three sedimentary basins under exploration, which are:

- the coastal basin : 6,000 Km$^2$
- the central basin : 800,000 Km$^2$
- the western section of the
  East African Rift system : 50,000 Km$^2$

The basin in the East African Rift system comprises the Albertine Graben (or depression), the Semliki Plain, Lake Edward, together with the Tanganiyika, the Upemba and the Banguelo Grabens.

The petroleum potential in DRC is both offshore and onshore. Private partnerships associated with the State via the national oil company, *la Congolaise des Hydrocarbures* (COHYDRO) carries out the exploration.

Studies to evaluate the oil potential have identified six interesting prospects. Their potential is estimated at over 4.5 billion barrels of oil.

Reserves of asphalt limestone and sand in Mavuma, on the eastern border of the coastal basin, have been estimated as follows:

- actual reserves     :     14,531,000 tons
- potential reserves  :     800,000,000 tons.

To summarise, offshore oil represents 115 million barrels and that onshore 22 million, hence total reserves of 137 million barrels.

Associated gas reserves are estimated at 20 billion $m^3$ offshore and 10 billion $m^3$ onshore, hence a total of 30 billion $m^3$ of gas.

In spite of all this potential, current production is scarcely 25,000 barrels per day and is concentrated exclusively in the Atlantic area (Lower-Congo Province), 15,000 barrels of which are onshore and 10,000 offshore. DRC is ranked in 68th place amongst the oil-producing countries. Revenue earned from this production varies between 200 and 300 million dollars per year.

The creation of Mutual Interest Zones (ZIC *Zones d'Intérêts Communs*) with Angola should have been worth more than 600 million dollars, according to the estimates given by the Minister for Hydrocarbons[222]. In addition to this, the adoption of the law on maritime territorial waters encourages the granting of licences for exploration and exploitation on the continental shelf.

With respect to the oil deposits discovered in Lake Albert (the Albertine Graben) in common ownership with Uganda, the first geophysical, seismic and gravimetric studies have been completed and surface indicators identified. However, to-date, no drilling has been carried out in the Congolese part of the Tanganyika, Albertine and Edward Grabens. In contrast, the Canadian company Heritage Oil is already exploiting petroleum in the Ugandan zone.

There is a danger in this due to the fact that the petroleum from the bottom of the lake does not have any watertight boundary separation. Exploitation on the other side of the border could prove to be unfavourable to DRC's interests over time, if it does not act with due diligence and start the exploitation on its own side.

---

[222] Cf. *Le Potentiel* of 5 November 2009.

Lake Tanganyika, common to Burundi, DRC, Tanzania and Zambia is also brimfull of petroleum. For its part, Burundi has already granted exploitation licences to British Petroleum's SureStream Junior, South African Mineral Resources Corp. and to Terra Seis International[223]. It is in the interest of DRC which owns the largest part of the lake to follow close on the heels of Burundi, especially since, as has been said above, petroleum blocks do not have watertight boundary separation.

In the Central Basin, the Brazilian company HRT-Petroleum will be committing over 50 million dollars to an evaluation of the oil deposits[224].

With regard to methane gas, Lake Kivu holds an enormous amount together with the carbon dioxide dissolved in the water. Reserves have been estimated at 65 billion and at 250 billion $Nm^3$ respectively. In the opinion of the experts, Lake Kivu refills with gas at an average rate of 350 million $Nm^3$ per year. This rate has increased to 350 million $Nm^3$ per year over the past 15 years to the point where it represents a potential danger for the local residents if this gas is not exploited.

The studies available show that one site with 29 $km^3$ of methane gas is easy to exploit but this is more difficult with another with 22.3 $km^3$.

In spite of the existence of mutual exploitation projects between two member countries of the ECGLC, Rwanda has already started to exploit the gas in Lake Kivu which it shares with DRC.

Gas development is an open-ended market for many requirements such as the production of electricity, gas for domestic (cookers) and industrial (boilers) use. Rapid exploitation of Lake Kivu's methane gas would certainly enable electrification of some towns in the East of the country and in neighbouring countries as well as the production of fertiliser for agriculture[225].

---

[223] *Ibid.*

[224] Agence congolaise de Presse, 10 September 2008.

[225] Cf. The presentation of Professor G. BEYA SIKU, Vice-Minister for Hydrocarbons "Mise à jour du secteur congolais des hydrocarbures. Potentialités et opportunitiés d'investissement" during the IPAD (Infrastructure partnership for African Development) conference from 6 to 8 October 2009. Grand Hotel, Kinshasa DRC.

DRC's Parliament is focused on reform of the Hydrocarbon Code[226]. It will certainly need expertise from companies in countries around the Atlantic (Canada, USA, France, Brazil, etc.) in order to explore and exploit its petroleum to full advantage. It goes without saying that the acquisition of substantial oil revenue will benefit the country and help it improve the current economic situation: "The majority of emerging countries in Africa are oil producers: Angola, Nigeria... They can make use of the proceeds from oil sales for the vital part of their respective national budgets. When will DRC wake up? "[227]

## b. Hydroelectric dams

DRC's energy sector is characterised by a paradox; the country is endowed with abundant resources (particularly with a hydroelectric potential that could meet the needs of the entire African continent), but consumption is amongst the weakest in the world. DRC is an energy "disgrace" because of its rich hydrography which gives it a hydroelectric potential estimated at 100,000 MW, or 13% of worldwide hydroelectric potential. The total energy capacity installed is in the order of 2,516 MW, or 2.5% of the total potential. The Inga Dam is the main source of hydroelectric energy production. The two active power stations have a capacity of 1,775 MW. The construction of Inga III (4,000 MW) is included in the WESTCOR (Western Power Corridor) Project: Inga-Angola-Namibia-Republic of South Africa-Botswana[228].

The construction of Inga IV, whose cost is estimated at 5.66 billion dollars, will increase the site's capacity to 40,000 MW, or twice that of the Three Gorges dam in China and more than the whole of the national electrical production of South Africa. Hence the Inga Dam could produce electricity not only for several countries on the African continent but also for countries in southern Europe[229].

---

[226] See BAKANDEJA wa MPUNGU, G., *Droit minier de des hydrocarbures en Afrique centrale*, Kinshasa/Brussels, Afrique éditions – Larcier 2009.

[227] Cf. *Le Potentiel* of 5 November 2009.

[228] National Electric Company, Keynote plan for development of the electricity sector, 2005.

[229] Cf. African Development Bank, *Economic perspectives in Africa*, 2006/2007, p. 239; *The Independent* of 25 August 2009.

With, as mentioned above, a national exploitable potential of 100,000 MW distributed throughout the territory, it is surprising that only 2.5% of this potential has been developed. Whilst the available capacity is estimated at 14,500 GWH, the effective production is only 6000 to 7000 GWH. The *Société national d'Électricité* (SNEL), or National Electric Company, has a network with 5,511 km of HV lines, 4,470 km of MV and 17, 433 km of LV lines.

The facilities for the production, transport and distribution of SNEL's electricity are currently in a very advanced state of dilapidation, due notably to:

- The fact that more than half the generators installed in the interconnected hydroelectric power stations and others in individual power stations are at a standstill because of technical faults, with severe damage over several years, the unavailability of spare parts, the cannibalisation of equipment and insufficient maintenance;
- lack of civil engineering work and electromechanical equipment;
- Sedimentation of the channels feeding into the hydroelectric power stations, especially at Inga I and II;
- Saturation of the existing networks for the transport and distribution of electrical power;
- Bad state of repair and obsolescence of the high voltage apparatus and the equipment for measurements, control and protection;
- Overloading of equipment encouraging early ageing;
- Stoppage of diesel heat generators because of difficulties with the supply of oil products and the unavailability of spare parts[230].

In addition to these factors there is the non-payment by the State of its invoices for electricity consumption which amount to more than 400 million USD, bad management, the corruption and lack of motivation of badly paid personnel.

---

[230] For more information, see the Democratic Republic of the Congo, Ministry for Planning, *Programme minimum de partenariat pour la transition et la relance en RDC*, November 2004.

This situation results in:

- A very weak 1.4% of penetration (ratio between towns electrified and those identified);
- A derisory 6% distribution rate (ratio between households with and without electricity);
- An unreliable electricity supply;
- Recourse to other sources of energy, especially wood which represents 75% of energy consumption in the country, causing an untoward and massive deforestation[231].

The result of this is that for the energy sector to be a catalyst for development, it must be included amongst the priorities for the Congolese leaders, through an adequate institutional framework, legislation complying with international norms and a planned and rigorous management of the available resources.

In a more general context and beyond the African Continent, the Inga site must be considered as a quintessential tricontinental cooperation project in the field of energy. This is particularly true since a hydroelectric dam has the advantage of being non-polluting.

*c.  Water*

DRC possesses vast resources of water. Almost the entire territory is covered by the complex River Congo system, including several rivers of varied importance and also interior and cross-border lakes. Besides the current domestic, agricultural and industrial usage of watercourses, this hydrographical system provides a vast logistical network for the transport of persons and goods. The abundance of water resources above and below ground is such in DRC that they are estimated at 53% of the freshwater supply available in Africa. This contrasts with the low distribution rate with only 20% of the entire country supplied with water.

In rural areas, nearly 70% of the facilities in the existing system of water production and distribution (springs, wells and bores) are not in operation, due to lack of maintenance but also as a result of destruction caused during the various wars.

---

[231]  Cf. Keynote plan for development of the electricity sector.

121

If it is a fact that DRC has abundant freshwater resources available, it is equally true that to conserve and above all exploit this resource for the wellbeing of its people and the rest of the continent, it has major challenges to overcome including the need for substantial investments, which must take account of the following criteria:

– galloping demographic increase (the current population could triple between now and 2050);
– the rural exodus exacerbated by wars and leading to overpopulation in urban areas disrupting the planning, especially in respect to drinking water and adequate sanitation;
– pollution of drinking water sources by mining and industrial activity and the invasion of the catchment areas by urban populations, with harmful repercussions on the ecosystems and health;
– climate change and its impact on water resources.

At continental level, it is feared that pressure from the international community, faced for example with the drying out of Lake Chad and the advance of two deserts, the Sahara from the North and the Kalahari from the South, requires enforceable solutions for which DRC is not prepared.

Some analysts even claim that access to water may become the next *casus belli* between DRC and its neighbours, as in the case of access to strategic minerals.

In this context, DRC's membership of several regional bodies like the Economic Community of Central African States (ECCAS), the Southern African Development Community (SADC), *la Commission Internationale du Bassin Oubangui Shari* (CICOS) or International Commission for the Oubangui Shari Basin, International Conference on the Great Lakes Region (CIRGL), Nile Basin Initiative (NBI) and Lake Tanganyika Authority (LTA), is opportune because water may be used to promote regional cooperation and peace.

Hence the effective management of this resource becomes a major necessity for DRC in order to ensure its security first of all and that of others thereafter.

This resource may also offer a unique opportunity as a basis for the socio-economic development of DRC and the rest of the African continent.

This is possible due to the principle of profit-sharing in all the sectors affected by water, e.g. agriculture, energy, tourism, etc. Hence this means that DRC is obliged to reflect carefully upon its participation in these sectors, in order for it to influence the political agenda on water of all those who are interested in water potential, and in the objective of promoting peace.

The other domain concerned by water is the development of agriculture, animal husbandry and industry. In fact, a nation can only achieve development by maximising the added value in the primary, secondary and tertiary sectors. Water, at this stage is of utmost importance, since the operation of all extraction and production activities, even the transformation and preservation of agricultural, livestock or mining products, all depend on it. Water in the DRC may even be the driving force for this "added value" revolution, which will make other sectors more secure and so the effects will spill over the entire African continent.

All in all, water management requires key prerequisites from the Congolese leaders which are: peace, good governance, the reinforcement of human and technical capabilities and access to funds.

## 2. Mining

DRC is a "geological scandal" with more than 1,100 different mineral substances[232]. Its main minerals are copper, cobalt, coltan, manganese, cassiterite, gold, bauxite, chrome, nickel, germanium, uranium, etc., plus a variety of precious stones like marble, diamonds, malachite, turquoise, tanzanite, emeralds, etc.

Ores are so abundant that each province has its own mineral substances in sufficient volume to ensure its own development, although the Central Basin has not yet been the target for more intensive exploration.

The principal mining resources by province are as follows[233]

diamonds:             East Kasai, West Kasai, Bandundu, Equator, Eastern Province;

---

[232]  Cf. World Bank document, Democratic Republic of the Congo. *Good governance in the mining sector as a factor for growth*, October 2007, p. 20
[233]  Cf. Presentation of the geological map of the DRC, Mining Registry, Ministry for Mines, DRC, January 2010; BAKANDEJA wa MPNGU, G., *Droit minier...*, *op. cit.*

| | |
|---|---|
| gold: | Eastern Province, Maniema, Katanga, Lower Congo, North Kivu, South Kivu, Equator; |
| copper: | Katanga; |
| tin: | Katanga, North-Kivu, Maniema; |
| colombite tantalite (coltan): | North Kivu, South Kivu, Maniema, North Katanga; |
| bauxite | Lower-Congo; |
| iron: | Banalia, Katanga, Luebo, Eastern Kasai; |
| manganese: | Katanga, Lower-Congo; |
| coal: | Katanga; |
| petroleum: | Lower-Congo (Moanda coastal basin), Bandundu (Central Basin), Eastern Province (Ituri), Province of South-Kivu and Katanga (Lake Tanganyiks), Katanga (Lake Moero); |
| methane gas: | North-Kivu and South-Kivu (Lake Kivu); |
| oil shale: | Lower-Congo (Mvuzi); |
| cobalt: | Katanga; |
| nickel-chrome: | Western Kasai and Eastern Kasai, etc. |

The Catholic bishops in DRC, during a reading on the exploitation of natural resources in their country, made the following observation: "Instead of helping the development of our country and benefiting our people, ores, petroleum and forestry have become the causes of our misfortune." This observation recalls the key challenge which is "the well ordered and controlled exploitation of our natural resources"[234].

The mining sector which was in the past at the heart of DRC's economy has now become obsolete. Previously, around the 1980s, the GECAMINES produced half a million tons of copper annually and provided as much as 70% of the State's budget; nowadays, it only produces 22,000 tons of copper, or even less, per year. According to a recent study by the World Bank, tax revenue received from the mining

---

[234] Message from the National Episcopal Conference of the Congo, *CENCO*, 7 July 2007, n° 8.

companies amounted to 26.7 million USD in 2005 and 11.7 million USD in 2006.

According to the forecasts from the same source, the gross value of mining production will vary between 2 and 2.7 billion USD annually and the tax revenue between 186 and 388 million USD annually, from 2008 to 2017[235].

These receipts could increase if, and only if, this sector was cleaned up and well managed. In fact, the reduction in the tax revenue from the mining sector is mainly due to the following factors:
—  the illegal traffic in precious materials;
—  fraudulent practices and especially corruption in companies and public services;
—  lack of transparency in the negotiation and granting of mining rights;
—  conflicts of interests between agents from the State and those from political authorities;
—  lack of feasibility studies on mining deposits;
—  under-valuation of the deposits registered;
—  flagrant violation of the Code and Mining Rules;
—  selling short the interest of the State during the organisation of joint ventures with private enterprises.

Anarchy in the mining sector is such that it casts doubts on the fundamental principles of justice, legality, respect for local populations and the environment. In short, it even endangers the very sovereignty of the State[236].

Various well-researched reports have denounced all these irregularities and even sometimes named the perpetrators[237]. Resolution 1754 of the UN Security Council of 15 May 2007 establishes a direct link between the illegal exploitation of natural resources and the wars and

---

[235]  World Bank document, *op. cit.*, p. 32.
[236]  Cf. Message of the Permanent Committee of the National Episcopal Conference of the Congo, 9 February 2008, n° 9.
[237]  Cf. http://www.freewebs.com/congo-kinshasa/,Rapports: Report of the LUTUN-DULA Commission on the pillage of mining resources, Transitional National Assembly, Kinshasa, 2006; UN Experts' report on the illegal exploitation of the natural resources of the Democratic Republic of the Congo.

insecurity in DRC, facts established by a UN Group of experts between 2002-2003 and the LUTUNDULA Report in July 2005.

In DRC, writes Professor Ferdinand MUHIGIRWA Rusembuka, S.J. "the first African world war in 1998 is intrinsically linked to the illegal exploitation and systematic pillage of the natural resources of our country. This first African world war involved nine African countries in the war: DRC, Rwanda, Uganda, Burundi, Angola, Zimbabwe, Chad, Namibia and Eritrea"[238].

From then on the heartfelt cry of Monsignor Nicolas Djomo LOLA, Bishop of Tshumbe (Eastern Kasai) and CENCO President who declared during the 6th assembly of the "African Synod": "We deplore the fact that the international community is not doing enough to put an end to these wars and the violence nor paying sufficient attention to their real causes: the looting of natural resources. It restricts itself to taking care of the consequences of the wars instead of decisively attacking their causes in a convincing way."[239]

After the great crisis of 2008-2009, we are now participating in an upturn in the world economy marked by a increase in the prices of raw materials, including that of copper. A question that may be raised is whether, once more, DRC will be taking advantage of the opportunities offered by the boom on the international market.

This chapter cannot be wound up without making allusion to the "revisitation of the mining contracts", an expression much used lately in Congolese vocabulary.

In effect, the past few years have been marked by the process of revising mining contracts. A long process which, it has to be admitted, has politically and economically disappointed its supporters, both inside and outside the country. The noble mission assigned to it at the beginning has not resisted being worn down by time. It has unavoidably shrunk, and become a nightmare for the Congolese economy, causing an incomprehension which is disadvantageous to the entire Republic, especially for its traditional partners.

---

[238] MUHIGIRWA, R., "Bonne gouvernance et secteur minier en RD Congo", *Congo Afrique* n° 439, November 2009, p. 683.
[239] Vatican City, *News*, 8 October 2009.

Therefore, it is DRC's task to assume responsibility for its part in this failure, so as not to give the world the impression that it is like Jean-Paul Sartre's character who always thought hell was on the other person's doorstep. Facing up to this fact will enable the country to learn its lesson, then to turn to an intelligent and economically viable management of its mining potential, helped by partnerships agreed on a "win-win" basis. This recognition will also offer fresh perspectives in terms of new jobs, substantial revenues, in short, an improvement in Congolese social conditions due to the injection of the substantial new capital that the country needs. For no one can deny that the mining sector requires heavy investments.

In spite of the environment that still needs to be cleaned up, there is cause to be glad about the presence of specific important partners like the American Freepoort-McMoran which is making remarkable investments in the Tenke Fungurume Mining project in Katanga, Canadian companies such as First Quantum Ltd. and a group of Chinese companies.

However, it is also appropriate to emphasise that certain partners who may attempt to succeed by unofficial means will find themselves in difficulty with Congolese law and so make a "revisitation" inevitable.

The monogamous marriage of the Congolese economy with the mining sector, put to the test by the international financial crisis, has amply shown the country that the time has come to diversify its resources to achieve peaceful development. Hence it is important to turn to the particular opportunities offered by the agricultural, live-stock and environmental sectors.

## 3. Agriculture, livestock farming and fisheries

*a. Agriculture*

In the eyes of some observers, DRC is not only a geological but also an agricultural scandal. According to a study conducted jointly by the FAO, UNFPA and IIASA (1984), and as mentioned by E. TOLLENS, "If the Zaire of the time (now the DRC) had the same level of input as Belgium for example, it could feed about half the world's population which in the year 2000 will be some six billion inhabitants"[240].

---

[240] TOLLENS, E., "Le développement agricole et rural au Zaïre", *La revue nouvelle,*1989, p. 167.

This means that the potential is so enormous. The climatic conditions and its position straddling the equator give DRC the chance to be productive all year round unlike the alternating North and South, and without any need for irrigation[241].

And yet, despite these opportunities and the fact that agriculture has been declared "the priority of all priorities", agricultural production is stagnating.

In effect, although it exported agricultural produce twenty years ago, the country is now experiencing a deficit in production and must turn to imports to feed its population.

These ever increasing imports mainly concern a few basic food items: maize, rice, wheat, and livestock products[242].

There now needs to be an appreciable increase in production to meet everybody's requirements. For evidence has shown that no country can lay claim to development without solving the food problem beforehand. Agricultural production must be revitalised, especially food-producing agriculture. This principally concerns traditional agriculture in the country and therefore the policy for the sector should include appropriate measures to be implemented.

Peasant agriculture is comprised of family smallholdings with a maximum of one or two hectares available and producing more than 90% of the population's basic food[243].

This form of farming is characterised by extensive use of land, hence incorporating little chemical input. Moreover, women carry out 90% of the work in the fields[244].

It should be noted however that this sector has suffered in the past few decades from a total lack of credit to sustain the activity of these peasant women and female market gardeners. We recall that this local

---

[241] KANKWENDA MBAYA, "Le paradoxe de la crise agricole au Zaïre", in Le Zaïre, vers quelles destinées?, Ed. CODESRIA, Dakar, 1992, p. 307.
[242] KAZADI TSHAMALA, "Mutations structurelles de l'agriculture et la question paysanne au Zaïre", La revue nouvelle, special issue, March 1989, p. 157.
[243] TOLLENS, E., op. cit., p. 174.
[244] KIKA MAVUNDA, "Les freins culturels au développement de l'agriculture du Zaïre", Cahiers économiques et sociaux, vol. XXIII, special issue, December 1989, p. 164.

production is not enough, and the country is currently more than 70 % dependent on imported produce.

One of the approaches suggested to increase this production is to take inspiration from the successful experience of Professor YUNUS and establish an agricultural micro finance system for these small producers who can then organise a cooperative or any other kind of association[245].

Moreover, thanks to the vastness of its arable land and the abundance of its water distribution potential, DRC has a mission to become the agricultural heart and lungs of Africa. It is no hidden secret that all countries currently industrialised, whether Japan, the United Stated, South Korea, Canada, Brazil or European Union countries, first experienced great agricultural development which then acted as a springboard for their economic take-off.

Abundant and cheap food and an agricultural surplus, the export revenue from which can be reinvested in other sectors of the economy, are a sound base for any development.

Agriculture is the only sector which at the current time is likely to create much employment, whilst generating income able to sustain development in other sectors of the economy. We should not forget that agricultural development inevitably affects the poorest and less-advantaged members of society, and would then help improve their standard of living. With a Gross Domestic Product of less than 180 USD per citizen in 2008, and with its rural population comprising over 70 % of its citizens, DRC views agriculture as a principal answer to the problem.

Seventy-four per cent of the country's active population work in the primary sector, 59 % of which are in agriculture. Paradoxically, 92 % of Congolese households are affected by food insecurity. Yet DRC's environment offers enormous agro-pastoral, forestry and fishery potential, under-exploited to a large extent. For instance, the fishery potential that the hydrographic system can accommodate is estimated at more than 70 million tons annually, making it an important element in food security[246].

---

[245] YUNUS, M. et JOLIS, A., *Vers un monde sans pauvreté, l'autobiographie du "banquier des pauvres"*, Paris, publisher Jean-Claude Lattès, 1997.
[246] Ministry for Agriculture and Rural Development, 1998.

This now begs the question of how did agriculture develop during the colonial period and after independence.

During the colonial period, Belgium made considerable efforts to develop agricultural enterprises, with produce exclusively for export and to cover the needs of agro-industrial enterprises over the entire colony.

After the First World War, the colonial authority at first took an interest in traditional farming in order to supply the mining centres with food products. This resulted in the policy of obligatory cultivation of specific farm produce, in parallel with agrarian reform based on the listing of villagers in peasant groups. The role of the agricultural monitors during this policy was crucial to achieve the imposed quotas, through fines and bodily punishments.

The colonial government also implemented the policy of credit for the acquisition of agricultural material and equipment, the processing and marketing of agricultural produce to private companies which, in return, contributed towards the development of socio-economic infrastructure such as roads, schools and dispensaries.

The prosperity thus created in the agricultural sector enabled the amount of produce for export to increase, completely under colonial control, and to offer a structure for the country's economic expansion.

Hence, two types of produce could be distinguished, on one hand, industrial agricultural products destined for export (rubber tree, coffee, palm oil, sugar cane, cocoa, tea, cotton, etc.) which the colonials had the exclusive right to exploit; and on the other, the cultivation of produce for local consumption, whose production basically returned to the indigenous population (maize, tropical fruits, cassava, beans, bananas, etc.).

These crops were the subject of studies to improve their quality, the fight against parasites and other diseases affecting plants, the improvement in cultivation methods by the *Institut National pour les Etudes et la Recherche Agronomiques du Congo* (INERA) (or the National Institute for Agronomic Study and Research in the Congo), an institute provided with a substantial budget[247].

---

[247] *Programme national de Relance du Secteur agricole et rural 1997-2001*, Volume 1: Programme National, November 1997, pp. 1-2.

After the Congo's independence, the agriculture sector suffered a large downturn, and considerable losses were recorded by the plantations, livestock farmers, agro-industrial enterprises and at INERA outposts.

Various measures were announced and undertaken by successive governments to turn the agricultural sector around and thus initiate development in the rural community, but with no obvious signs of success.

For instance:

- the "Zairianisation" in 1973 of agricultural, commercial and transportation enterprises belonging to foreigners;
- nationalisation of the majority of companies and the creation of parastatal offices;
- return of "Zairianised" and nationalised companies to former owners in 1976;
- Provisional Plan for Agricultural Revival: 1966-1972;
- *Programme Agricole Minimum (PAM)* (or Minimum agricultural programme): 1980-1981;
- Plan for Agricultural Revival: 1982-1984;
- *Programme d'Autosuffisance Alimentaire (PRAAL)* (or Self-sufficiency in food programme): 1987-1990;
- Provisional Programme for Economic Rehabilitation;
- Five-Year Plan for Economic and Social Development: 1985-1990;
- Guidelines for Agricultural and Rural Development: 1991-2000;
- *Programme National de Relance du Secteur Agricole et Rural* (PNSAR) (or the national programme for revival of the agricultural and rural sector), 1997-2001;
- Three-Year Programme of support to Agricultural Sector Producers: 2000-2003[248].

In general, none of these plans or programmes could deliver a clear response to food security, or help eradicate poverty.

---

[248] Cf. *Programme minimum de partenariat pour la transition et relance en RDC*, p. 165.

It is a fact that these plans or agricultural development programmes had to face up to a multitude of constraints:

- the consequences of "Zairianisation which led to disinvestment and a lack of confidence by private investors, especially the foreign ones;
- infrastructure in a perpetual state of decay restricting access to markets and to basic social services;
- difficulties in the supply of improved seeds, good quality breeding stock, veterinary and fishery equipment and materials;
- lack of command of the techniques for conservation, processing and stockage of agricultural and the resulting considerable losses after harvesting;
- collapse of the system for supervising farmers;
- constant conflicts over land;
- difficult access to financial services;
- the dilapidation of agricultural service routes, etc.

Agriculture has very widely suffered from recent wars, with the accompanying pillage, insecurity in the countryside, impossibility to move around and the general breakdown of structures in the sector. It has even decreased to a level below subsistence. During the past decade, it has receded by 15%, whilst the population has increased at the rate of 3% per year. Export income in the sector has fallen drastically following the abandonment of industrial crops. The small agricultural undertakings have no capital. The middle class is practically no longer represented in this sector. Some of the large national investors were looted before and during the wars. Many years will be needed before the sector can turn itself around and recapitalise. Imports destined to fill the gap between supply and demand have considerably increased[249].

Despite the substantial potential of this sector, budgetary credits granted to agriculture and to rural development remain extremely weak, and represent scarcely 1.5% of the Republic's Budget.

The small degree of political will that successive governments have shown towards agriculture, although continually claimed to be a

---

[249] Cf. *Le Potentiel*, "Autopsie du secteur agricole de la République démocratique du Congo", edition 3116 of 2 May 2006.

"priority amongst priorities" in official speeches, has not encouraged private players to invest in this sector.

From now on, how can investments in this sector be encouraged in DRC? It must be assumed that agricultural and economic development will move towards internal reorganisation in the medium term and towards integration in the regional economy and the liberalization of trade in the long term. It is thus important to give agriculture references as explicit as the Mining and Forestry Codes or the Land Code, by establishing an Agricultural Code which will particularly include details on the competent authority and the guidelines to agricultural taxation, the corresponding specifications or even the rights and obligations of those involved.

DRC is a country with a vocation for agriculture and where, as a reminder, over 70% of its population live in a rural environment and depend mainly on agricultural activity. The potential in this sector predisposes it to play an important part in the socio-economic development of the country. Although its contribution towards GDP has been 30%, 34%, 52%, and 49.5% respectively in 1985, 1990, 1995 and 2005, the relative significance of which is not justified by the performances of the sector itself but rather by the collapse of the production from manufacturing industry and extractive mining[250].

According to E. TOLLENS, "It is true that mining and forestry development may generate more income for the State and may be the origin of strong economic growth, but this will be an economic development with no real 'development' benefiting the entire population". And relatively little means are needed to restart the agricultural sector and for it to make a significant contribution to economic growth: a favourable macroeconomic framework, the free movement of goods and people, an improvement in the transport infrastructure, production of quality seeds, minimum supervision of peasants, etc."[251].

---

[250] Cf. Programme minimum de partenariat pour la transition et la relance en RDC.
[251] TOLLENS, E., "L'état actuel de la sécurité alimentaire en RD Congo: diagnostic et perspectives", a communication given to the conference on food security in the DRC, FAO/Kinshasa, 18 February 2003, p. 53.

On this basis, a few priority measures may be singled out for the revival of the agricultural sector in DRC:

" – Invest massively in the refurbishment of the means of communication, by river, land, or rail to permanently open up the country's interior and hence link the production area with the consumer centres (usually the urban areas);

– Implement a credit system adapted to requirements, in favour of associations of producers and centres for agricultural players (micro-credits, agricultural cooperatives); limit policies for the free distribution of goods and materials, for they run counter to the development process;

– Initiate a programme to encourage crops for export, taking due account of comparative advantages;

– Firmly encourage humanitarian agencies to obtain food supplies locally for basic needs (maize, rice, beans, cassava, groundnuts, sugar and oil), reduce the scope of action under the humanitarian assistance policy itself to only those people made vulnerable by natural catastrophes and conflicts;

– Apply legislative and regulatory provisions, levying reduced taxes and customs dues for input material and agricultural equipment; simplify local agricultural taxation (by decentralising the administrative authorities); instigate an Agricultural Code with an incentive-based tax and customs system; and reduce the cost of electricity and diesel (agricultural fuel);

– Revise the law on land in order to reinforce the protection and guarantees to private owners against theft, looting and other land infringements;

– Grant all economic player the licence to create and maintain supply routes or main roads, together with, and if need be, to participate in the renovation of the railways, even if it means applying compensatory measures elsewhere;

– Favour or encourage the creation of infrastructure for commercial activities insofar as the private sector is not able to do so;

– Promote national production, favour the provincial and territorial organisation of agriculture and craft exhibitions designed to promote the best agricultural produce and best animal breed; reward the best farm and rural operators;

- Create a Chamber for Agriculture;
- Strengthen measures to protect the environment and basic natural production;
- Reinforce the production capacity of small producers and vulnerable groups by giving them easier access to the means of production in the short term to enable them to reduce the contraints they face. This means making access easier to quality seeds, and cuttings resistant to disease and harmful insects;
- Improve the basic agricultural services, the support infrastructure for production and marketing to make the production sites more viable and to reduce losses after harvesting;
- Eliminate the artificial barriers to domestic trade all the way down the food chain, to connect the small farmers to markets; this means the elimination of administrative obstacles to transport and to trade in agricultural goods and produce;
- The agricultural sector does not benefit from funds likely to allow it to play the role attributed to it for economic and social development. To this end, the drafting of the guidelines for expenditure in this sector in the medium term should be finalised, so that the government will rapidly have information available for budgetary planning. This information will thus enable the government to make the budgetary adjustments which take account of the Maputo Declaration, i.e. devoting 10 % of the State's budget to the agricultural sector;
- Draft a decentralisation plan which incorporates detailed programmes for agricultural and rural development at provincial level and organise studies on such topics as the diversification of the channels for agricultural exports, development of animal and fish production, land regulations, promotion of rural financial intermediation and of the micro-enterprise in order to strengthen food security and fight poverty. To achieve this, an exchange and compilation of information between the principal players in the sector should be carried out within the provincial agricultural Councils to be established;
- Implement an agricultural information system and conduct appropriate studies to act as a basis for decision-making by public authorities, the private sector and civil society;
- Find the mechanisms to improve the working conditions of public service officials (supervisors, teachers, researchers, etc.) with

decent salaries and suitable equipment for work; promote and strengthen the professional agricultural organisations; revitalise the schools, universities and training centres in the agricultural, livestock, fishing, industrial, small-scale undertaking and agro-food processing sectors;

– Adequately target food aid; the government and partners should ensure that this aid does not have a negative impact on the production and consumption of local agricultural produce;

– Rapidly establish a Code for Agriculture. This instrument will give equal access to all farmers to land assets. It will enable the dualism between land law and ways and customs to be reduced, and also ensure the protection of private agricultural property against theft and pillage. It will give security to trade in seeds and will indicate the attraction of this sector;

– Create an Agricultural Registry which will, henceforth, be responsible for the management of the land scheduled for agriculture and for agricultural buildings. This body will also be responsible for updating the national agricultural map, which indicates the location of every farmer, large or small. This will be an essential database for well-conducted agricultural planning, needed for a real revival of agriculture."[252]

Several potential areas for agricultural development are worthy of consideration at this point.

The evaluation of factors like agricultural potential, access to markets and demographic pressure which interact with the various production areas in DRC will allow an identification of the potential areas for development or sectors in which a suitable agricultural strategy could have considerable positive effect.

Hence, by using the interactive guidelines based on a range of dichotomous "high" and "low" values for each variable, three potential areas have been identified which are:

(i) Regions with a high degree of agricultural potential, a high density population and wide access to markets;

---

[252] *Le Potentiel,* as mentioned above.

(ii) Regions with a high degree of agricultural potential, restricted access to markets and a low density of population and;

(iii) Regions with a low degree of agricultural potential, wide access to markets and a low density of population.

If we take the first field by way of illustration, five axes or regions have been identified:

- "**Axis 1:** Region extending from the Atlantic Ocean to Eastern Kasai (Kabinda) with the products to be developed; cassava, rice, groundnuts, beans, vegetables, banana, palm oil, cocoa, fish produce, cattle, cotton and sugar cane. This axis enjoys a comparative definite advantage for the rearing of large ruminants.

- **Axis 2:** Mining towns in the province of Katanga and their surrounding areas, with production to be developed: groundnuts, vegetables, cotton, sugar cane, large and small ruminants and aquaculture.

- **Axis 3:** Region of the Great Lakes of Africa, specially in the East of the Democratic Republic of Congo, from Pueto (Katanga) to Aru (Eastern Province) including North-Kivu and South-Kivu with the following production: cassava, maize, beans, plantains and vegetables. This axis has great potential for arabica coffee (cool climate with altitude) and a very great potential for cattle rearing, especially dairy cattle.

- **Axis 4:** The northern part of the Equator Province, with the following production, cassava, maize, rice, plantains, vegetables, coffee, cocoa, large and small ruminants. This axis also has potential for beekeeping, aquaculture and fishing.

- **Axis 5:** Regions from the Kisangani hinterland to Pool Malebo. This axis is located along the River Congo: fish products, cassava, maize, rice, groundnuts, plantains, vegetables, palm oil, cocoa and rubber tree. A good situation along the River Congo, the possibility to develop beekeeping in the Kisangani and Bumba hinterlands"[253].

Given the soil conditions and food habits, these axes may be supplemented with produce from specific provinces. This is why the produc-

---

[253] Cf. *Revue du secteur agricole, les filières de développement agricole en RDC par axes de développement*, Kinshasa, Ministry of Agriculture, 2004, pp. 58-63.

tion of maize in Katanga and in Western and Eastern Kasai, sugar cane in North- and South-Kivu and in the Eastern Province should be encouraged.

Traditionally, the main agricultural products in DRC are:

1. Food crops: cassava, maize, rice, pulses (groundnuts, beans, cowpea and soybean), bananas and plantain, market gardens (sweet potato, amaranthine, etc.) and other food crops such as wheat, sugar cane, potatoes, yams, etc.;
2. Industrial and perennial cultivation: cotton, rubber tree, oil palm, tea, coffee (arabica and robusta), cocoa, and cultivation for medicinal and industrial applications such as papaya (papain), quina (quinine) and rauwolfia (various components), used in the pharmaceutical industry.

This nonexhaustive list of names for DRC's agricultural products adequately shows the need for drafting and the importance of implementing an outline plan to reform agriculture, so as to meet the national and worldwide challenges of the current food crisis and to combat poverty.

*b.  Livestock*

With its great expanses of pasture and wooded savannah, DRC offers great opportunities for the development of animal husbandry. Yet, the country only has 1 to 1.3 million heads of cattle, although its pastoral potential is for 30 to 40 million heads of cattle. Livestock farmed includes small animals, cattle and poultry. Their percentages were estimated in 1997 to be 34% for pork, 24% goats, 22.3% cattle, 15% poultry and 3.9% sheep[254]. The potential is particularly large in the East of the country (Ituri, the two Kivu and North-Katanga). But the general poverty and the massive importation of low quality, frozen meat products at uncompetitive prices (about 1 USD per kg) hinder development in this sector. The keeping of small livestock and poultry has spread, particularly in urban and peripheral urban areas, where it is reared for home consumption and for sale in town.

---

[254]  PNSAR, 1997, abovementioned.

The main restriction to the development of animal husbandry in DRC lies in demand. The demand for meat produced locally has a high elasticity, as this produce is of good quality and so the cost is high in comparison with that for imported products. Moreover, the consumption of beef has greatly declined since 1975. According to studies on consumer spending, annual consumption of meat in Kinshasa (3.3 kg/inhabitant) has declined by 50 % since 1975, whilst that of fish (fresh and preserved, especially the mpiodi) has stabilised at 10-11 kg per inhabitant[255].

The best way to remedy the development of this sector would be strong and sustained economic growth, largely shared by the population.

Moreover, it should be noted that in the past, associations or cooperatives of breeders carried out disease prevention and veterinary care in the two Kivu and Ituru[256].

For social reasons, it is difficult to put the brake down hard on low-quality meat and fish imports at relatively cheap prices. However, some protection against these cheap imports is required if the local production of good or medium quality meat is to be encouraged. A similar protection already officially exists, but it is often circumvented by various means: procedure for emergency deliveries, transit procedure, false classification of products[257], etc.

Apart from the support services for developing animal farming (research, expansion, training, marketing support), the role of the State on the issue of stock rearing is above all:

– to regulate and ensure respect of the legislation in force regarding imports (customs duties and taxes) and hygiene checks;
– to supervise for hygiene purposes, the fight against epizootics and veterinary disease prevention (preventive treatment against parasites, fight against the Tsetse fly, vaccinations, etc.);

---

[255] TOLLENS, E., "Les défis: sécurité alimentaire et cultures de rente pour l'exportation. Principales orientations et avantages comparatifs de l'agriculture en RD Congo", Roundtable on Agriculture in the DRC, Kinshasa, 19-20 March 2004.
[256] *Ibid.* pp. 20-21.
[257] Eggs for normal consumption are imported from the Netherlands in the guise of eggs for hatching, exempt from any tax or customs dues.

–  to sustain and support scientific research in the field of animal farming and production to improve pedigrees;
–  to supervise the breeders' cooperatives.

This role is essential for a State, even in a free economy, as it is anywhere else in the world.

c.  *Fisheries*

Crossed by one of the most powerful rivers in the world, with large lakes, many rivers and other watercourses, DRC has all the principal advantages for fishing and associated industries.

When it became independent in 1960, the country inherited a certain amount of fishing infrastructure. During the first decade after independence, some fisheries benefited from significant funds for their development. Amongst others, they are at Moanda on the Atlantic Ocean in the Province of the Lower Congo, Vitchumbi on Lake Edward in the Province of North-Kivu, and Kalemie on Lake Tanganyika in the Province of Katanga.

The River Congo also has two large fishing ports at Kisangani and Mbandaka which are able to feed almost all the 10 million inhabitants of the capital, Kinshasa[258].

Alongside this activity of an industrial nature, small-scale fishing supplies the bulk of the fish consumed by the great majority of local populations. Without adequate installations for preservation or processing, the freshwater fish in the Congo are either sold in their natural state, or processed as smoked or salted fish.

The lack of investments and supervision in this sector has meant that since the 1980s the country has become an importer of mackerel of indeterminate nutritional quality.

At the same time, quality fish such as the Nile Perch, Tilapia, etc. are dying of old age in the rivers, lakes and streams in Congo.

With regard to the many opportunities and inland fish reserves which could guarantee an annual production of around 701,000 tons of fish, according to the statistics of the Ministry of Agriculture, DRC

---

[258]  *The Washington Post*, 2 November 2001.

could not only guarantee its food autonomy in this sector, but also export volumes of fish to other African countries at competitive prices.

Not only will the revival in this sector contribute to the strengthening of South-South cooperation, but it will also reduce to a minimum Africa's dependence upon other continents for this foodstuff.

## 4. Conservation and protection of environment

The worldwide struggle against global warming makes the management of a sustainable environment a priority on the agenda of all governments. The transnational nature of ecosystems and phenomena, and the action taken with an environmental impact requires international cooperation for efficient management of the environment. The cloud from Tchernobyl which went round the Earth several times, should remind us of the truth about the exceptional nature of our environmental destiny which is above and beyond national considerations. This awareness has resulted in the establishment of guidelines for the Multilateral Environmental Agreements (MEA), the most relevant concern the struggle against climatic change, management of biological diversity and the management of long-lasting organic pollutants.

Therefore, environmental matters have become a major issue which goes beyond purely national considerations[259]. The Atlantic region cannot shrink from the need for coordinated management of the environment, given such factors as: its maritime waters, forests, fauna at sea and on land, the human activities carried out, especially those in the forests, in the sea and underwater, the production, transport and elimination of dangerous waste, trade in protected species, management of shared resources, etc. Because of their similar concerns and the specific nature of ecological issues, various government and non-government players inside the region are working to find a framework for negotiations and collaboration on such matters as global warming, deforestation, the carbon market, control of the transportation of dangerous products, exportation of non-polluting products and industries, and the trade in protected species or those becoming extinct. This will enable

---

[259] See KAMTO, M., *Droit de l'environment en Afrique,* Paris, Édicef, 1996; KISS, A., *Droit international de l'environment,* Paris, Pedone, 1989; NEURAY, J.-F., *Droit de l'environment,* Brussels, Bruylant, 2001.

the different instruments conceived at world level to be revised to suit specific situations.

The vastness and diversity of the environmental resources in DRC make the country a strategic partner who should be at the centre of the international community's concerns about current ecological issues. Under-estimated statistics[260] indicate it has more than 60% of its forest area in the Congo Basin, which is between 120 and 140 million hectares out of its 230 million of tropical rainforests, the second largest forest area in the world after the Amazon, and of prime importance for climate regulation on land. With other land and forest ecosystems, the Congolese forests shelter a diversity of flora and fauna of great socio-cultural, economic and environmental interest, as much for its own people as for the whole of humanity. These forests represent 12.5% of the entire world's tropical rainforests and are equivalent to the total surface area of forests in all the European Union countries. It has the third largest area of national forest, after Brazil and Indonesia.

With the fourteenth largest river in the world in length and with several lakes on its territory, DRC is blessed with an important water heritage which is a vital environmental resource for the entire sub-region. These waters carry out important regulatory functions, notably in maintaining the atmospheric humidity and rainfall in the region, regulating the salinity in the estuary by discharging millions of cubic metres per second into the ocean, which is an essential role in conserving the coastal marine biodiversity.

Forty-one kilometres in length, DRC's Atlantic coast is exposed to three main sources of pollution, essentially exogenous: international shipping, activities to exploit the seabed and land-based marine pollution. International cooperation is necessary for better management of the Congolese coastal area in order to better protect the marine ecosystem. To this end, DRC is a party to the Abidjan Convention of 23 March 1981 relating to cooperation on the protection and enhancement of the marine environment and the coastal areas in the West and Central African Region, as well as the London Convention

---

[260] Cf. *Le Potentiel* n° 4776 of 12 November 2009; KASONGO NUMBI, *Les eaux et forêts de la RDCongo. Changement climatique de la planète, les enjeux*, Paris, L'Harmattan, 2007.

of 2 November 1973 on the prevention of pollution from shipping. It is also party to the Montego Bay Convention on the law of the sea of 10 December 1982.

## a. Forests

### Composition

DRC's forests are divided into four main categories: dense rainforest, mountainous forest, woodland (of the Miombo kind), and the savannah-forest mixture. The entire Congolese forests currently absorb a stock of carbon estimated at 40 Gigatons (Gt), or the equivalent of 150 Gt of potential $CO_2$ emissions, which would be the entire current worldwide emissions over more than six years.[261]

The forest as a whole currently plays a key socio-economic role in DRC; it covers almost 60% of the 234 million hectares that comprise its national territory; more than 90% of its current population, estimated at more than 60 million inhabitants, live in forest areas. Cutting down wood and processing it into charcoal supplies over 90% of domestic energy. The exploitation of wood from the forests makes a significant contribution to GNP. This exploitation is 60% small-scale and unofficial and plays a major part in sustaining the economy of rural households. Beside its use as domestic energy and wood for construction, the small-scale and informal sector is also active in the cross-border trade in wood, mainly in the eastern provinces of the Republic, in transit to the maritime ports in Kenya and Tanzania[262].

### Conservation of Congolese forest national heritage

Congo has a natural protection because the country is enclosed (with only 41 km of coastline located in the West) and most of it is inaccessible. Outside the Atlantic coastal area, this forest has been relatively well conserved from deforestation and damage, with a historical rate of

---

[261] *Forest Resource Management*, FAO, UNEP, 2005; DUVEILLER *et al.*, Deforestation in Central Africa: Estimates at Regional, National and Landscape Levels by Advanced Processing of systemically-Distributed Landsat Extracts", *Remote Sensing of Environment*, 112, Université catholique de Louvain, 2008, pp. 1969-1981.

[262] For more details, cf. VANDE WEGHE, J.P., *Forêts d'Afrique centrale, la nature et l'homme*, Tielt, 2004.

143

deforestation oscillating between 0.2 and 0.3% over the past 20 years. This is relatively modest in comparison with the worldwide average, estimated at 0.6% over the same period.

Together with the peat bogs and land convertible into secondary forests, which are also natural carbon wells, the mass of Congolese forests plays a key role in regulating climate. But population increases which will require more space for the construction and expansion of housing, the internal and external demand for food, wood products, fibres, energy, as well as the corresponding increase in the price of these products on the world market, seriously threaten the preservation of this great mass of forest. This may have a negative effective on its vital function as the lungs for humanity to absorb part of the excess carbon emitted into the atmosphere. However, the imperatives for economic growth, development and the fight against poverty may compel the Congolese government to play down the opportunities offered by the forest to achieve these objectives. The negotiations in progress to convert close to three million hectares of forested land into oil palm plantations to produce bio-fuels can be mentioned as one example. Currently, the Congolese forests are in the main protected by biophysical considerations and the modest economic interest that they are accorded, given the cost of the initial investments for their development, which saves them from small-scale exploitation. However, it is to be feared that the pressure exerted by the abovementioned factors will not be likely to make this natural protection disappear, through the use of low-cost technology but negative for the ecology and with the influx of substantial capital, as in the example already mentioned. Besides, the area protected by law is relatively small.

Nonetheless, there is a systematic institutional measure for preserving the forest's national heritage. This has been happening since the 1970s, when national parks and nature reserves [263] were created by the Ministry for the Environment, Nature Conservation and Tourism, through participation at several international gatherings as well as

---

[263] See Law n° 75/024 relating to creation of sectors protected of 26 July 1975. It allowed the creation of several national parks (Virunga, Kahuzi-Biega, Salonga, Upemba, Maïko, Garamba and Kundelungu); where rare species such as: elephants, hippotamus, zebras, okapis, mountain gorillas, bonobos, leopards, white rhinoceros, etc. are to be found.

ratification of international treaties on the environment[264]. The World Charter for Nature was adopted by the UN General Assembly (Res. 37/7) on 28 October 1982 on the initiative of the ex-Zaire. This institutionalised resolve is still continuing, and only mentioning the most outstanding initiatives, includes ratification of the COMIFAC (*Commission des Forets d'Afrique Centrale* or Commission for the Central African Forests) treaty, implementation of sub-regional directives on the active participation of local and indigenous people and non-governmental organisations in the management of the Central African forests, active participation in the FLEGT (Forest Law Enforcement, Governance and Trade) process – an initiative of the European Union aiming to improve the governance of forests –, activation of the process to create local community forests, membership of the RED, REDD and REDD+ process in which DRC is a pilot country, etc.

Also, should the institutionalised resolve of DRC be reinforced by the systematic and strategic evaluation of the environmental impact of the development programme and any project for development and investment? There has to a point of optimal balance between the sovereign necessity to achieve development and combat poverty and the paramount need to preserve the forest's national heritage, with its capital importance in the worldwide fight against climate change.

*REDD mitigation leverage*

The resolve of the Congolese government to become fully involved in the REDD (Reducing Emission from Deforestation and Forest Degradation in Developing Countries, a UN Programme) dates from the beginning of this process. At the 13th Conference of the Parties to the UN Framework Convention on Climate Change, held in Bali (Indonesia) from 3 to 14 December 2007, the Minister for the Environment, Nature Conservation and Tourism, in conjunction with the Woods Hole Research Center, submitted a report entitled "Reducing $CO_2$ emissions from deforestation and degradation in the Democratic Republic of Congo: a first look". In 2010, he confirmed and presented the public with the second version of his Preparation Plan for the REDD

---

[264] See MBALANDA KISOKA, *Receuil des textes juridiques en matière environnementale en République Démocratique du Congo*, Kinshasa, Justada, 2000.

during an academic session held on February 19. This programme will be integrated into the strategy for the socio-economic development of the country.

This process proved there was a vital need for more detailed studies to identify, categorise and evaluate the impact of the direct and indirect, past present and future motivations for the deforestation and degradation of the forests, to create realistic scenarios for the evolution curve of deforestation and degradation based on past data and an analysis of the motivations identified, to determine realistic strategies to reverse the curve and to set up a viable system for the observation, reporting and verification, to enable a better follow-up of the forest's evolution. The challenge faced by the government is in effect to anticipate the mitigation leverage which would permit conservation and an increase in the rate of deforestation in some Congolese forests, whilst making a positive contribution to national development and the eradication of poverty, which remain the government's priorities.

A few low cost mechanisms for REDD leverage mitigation[265], must be activated. These are:

"– reducing demand for wood for heating by promoting the use of improved ovens to some 5 million urban households, representing a 6% potential reduction, at a cost of €1.7t $CO_2$e as well as increasing the supply of wood for heating through many more reforestation and afforestation projects, equivalent to 3 or 4% of the potential reduction, at an average cost of 2 to 2.5 €/t $CO_2$e;

– the search for alternative domestic energy sources both in rural and urban areas, notably biofuels produced in small-scale peasant smallholdings on land outside the forest areas and of little use for agriculture;

– afforestation/reforestation projects to constitute new carbon wells representing 35% of the total potential for reduction and storage, could also be achieved at relatively low cost (35% of the potential,

---

[265] Cf. GRIFFITHS, T., MARTONE, F., Forest Peoples' Programme, Seeing 'REDD'? Forests, Climate Change Mitigation and the Rights of Indigenous Peoples and Local Communities, http://www.rightsand resources.org; DRC, UN Forum on the Forests, Ministry of the Environment, Nature Conservation, Water and Forests, *National Report*, Kinshasa, 2004.

somewhere between 1 and 1.6 €/t $CO_2$e for reforestation and 3 to 4.2 €/t $CO_2$e for afforestation);

– finally, programmes to improve the productivity of agriculture for food crops (supply of fertilisers and seeds, training, etc.) and for business (supply of fertiliser and seeds, training and accreditation of projects to organise networks for production and distribution) provide a significant potential for mitigation (4% and 16%, respectively) at costs lower than the average (about 6.5 €/t $CO_2$e and 4.85 €/t $CO_2$e, respectively).

## b. Land Wealth

This is the last strategic resource for humankind in the worldwide battle against climatic change. It is widely available in DRC: estimations vary between 100 and 200 million hectares of non-forested land, 70% of which is suitable for agriculture. There are over 4 million hectares of natural pasture, very little exploited.

The population density is very low: some 27 inhabitants per $km^2$, with large concentrations of people in a few urban centres the length of the non-mountainous area of the Great Lakes, whilst the rest of the country has a density lower than ten inhabitants per $km^2$. The country has even more vital space available to build more homes so it may sensibly handle demographic growth.[266]

An appropriate policy for the affectation of land may give this resource important leverage for mitigation. In fact, a plan to divide up the land would involve 20% for food production, 20% to create secondary forests, 20% for industrial cultivation, including 10% for the production of biofuels, which would still leave 40 million hectares of land in reserve, whilst at the same time making an appreciable effort to solve some immense problems on the world agenda, especially the food crisis, atmospheric pollution from the combustion of fossil fuels, and the fight against poverty at sub-regional level.

---

[266] Cf. *Institut National des Statistiques et des Études Économiques* (INSEE) (The French National Institute for Statistics and Economic Research), *Population, densité et part de la population urbaine des principaux pays du monde...Congo (République démocratique du Congo)*, www.insee.fr.

The national strategic approaches to development, around which a strategy to mobilise international cooperation should be formed, should incorporate the following objectives to develop this vast wealth of land:

"– the development of an agro-industry with a very small carbon footprint, characterised by the intensive use of organic fertilisers, an environmentally-friendly management of agricultural waste, optimum use of irrigation, the establishment of local facilities for transforming and improving the regional distribution chains;

– the production of biofuels for agricultural machinery and transport, whilst boosting the fleet of machinery and by completing the river network with rail for greater efficiency in the movement of incoming and outgoing materials and equipment;

– the creation of new carbon wells by establishing secondary forests".

### c. Global warming

The Congo's natural resources, comprising the forests, its water network and unforested land, constitute a precious environmental resource for Africa and humankind. It provides priceless ecological service; the forest's existence helps maintain abundant rainfall in the region, which flows into all the river basins that crisscross one another, including the Congo basin, the Nile Basin and the southern African water network, and mainly the network of tributaries of the River Congo and other major rivers. The Congolese river network, which includes the River Congo, the fourteenth longest in the world and with the second largest volume, has an economic and environmental importance: climate regulation, hydroelectricity production, clean renewable energy, and irrigating the soil. Finally, the Congo's land can enable both the capacity of carbon storage to be increased through the creation of secondary forests, and also the pollution from the combustion of fossil fuels to be reduced through the production of biofuels used for transport and agricultural machinery. This potential is crucial in the current state of affairs.

The various ecosystems in Congo are also home to a very large number of endemic species of flora and fauna, placing DRC amongst the leading group of countries with a mega-biodiversity.

With regard to the debate on global warming, international pressure should continue to be placed on the polluting countries so that they reduce the emission of greenhouse gases (GHG). This is the price to pay for saving the future of humanity. As far as possible, objectives for reducing GHG should be quantified, recorded and checked.

The financial and international support mechanisms incorporated in the framework of the various Multilateral Agreements on the Environment are not sufficient for the DRC's environmental potential. The huge problems preventing the realisation of this potential lie with the weakness in technology, the economy and institutions of the country which is emerging from a very long period of conflicts and general disorder. Given the sheer size of the potential that it possesses, Congo can justifiably claim to provide part of the solution to the world's climate problem. Hence it is necessary to conceive strategies and to formulate a specific plea that will result in the mobilisation of significant human and financial resources, and significant technology transfer, above and beyond that already designated by the various agreements to which the country is a signatory.

Political stability, internal security, the strengthening of the State's authority and improvement in economic and environmental governance in DRC should be the focus of the international community's preoccupations. This is the price to pay so all humanity can expect to take advantage of the enormous potential inherent in this country.

President Sarkozy's initiative to organise a meeting in Paris with the countries with the four great forest basins (Amazon, Congo, Indonesia and Siberia) is praiseworthy on more than one account[267]. DRC and Brazil, with the support of the other countries around the Atlantic, could adopt common positions on the conservation of tropical forests, also positions to be defended within other organisations like the UN, African Union and WTO, etc.

## 5. Infrastructure sectors and holding companies

### a. Infrastructure

The government's deficit, insufficient means and armed conflicts have resulted in the dilapidation, in both the capital and also the prov-

---

[267] The meeting as planned by President Sarkozy has not yet taken place, but it is an initiative to be encouraged.

inces, of infrastructure such as hospitals, schools, roads, railways, airports, stations, administrative buildings, etc.

For example, the transport network in DRC, in normal times, covers 16,238 navigable kilometres, with 5,033 km of rail track, 145,000 km of national and provincial roads as well as secondary rural tracks, 7,400 km of suburban roadways and 270 airports for the whole of the country, including five international airports (Kinshasa, Lubumbashi, Kisangani, Goma and Gbadolite)[268].

The major part if not the entire infrastructure needs to be completely or partly overhauled, to modernise and enable it to be truly operational. The transport networks, with few exceptions (airway network, river network, and road and railway networks in specific provinces) no longer provide the economic and social sectors with the infrastructure and services to help trade of any kind and to allow the movement of goods and people[269].

The public transport sector in the urban areas is characterised by the lack of involvement of the State, the unbridled increase in demand due to the rural exodus of people in the search for a better life and the massive presence of persons displaced inside the country through armed conflicts. The commercial situation and the dilapidated state of the roads do not encourage the economic players, apart from some independent initiatives, to commit large investments to this sector.

The adoption of an extensive and ambitious programme of infrastructure renovation and construction is required to modernise the country, improve people's welfare and give some impetus to the national economy.

The plan for renovation and reconstruction of the infrastructure will particularly emphasise the following features:

"– national, provincial and agricultural use roads;
– dredging of the river and its tributaries ("natural motorways");
– railways;

---

[268] Cf. DSCRP (document for the strategy on growth and poverty reduction), *op. cit.* P.34.
[269] Cf. MAVUNGU, J.-P., *De la mise en oeuvre d'une diplomatie de développement dans les relations entre la République démocratique du Congo et ses partenaires exté- rieurs*, Kinshasa, February 2007, p. 18, unpublished text.

- maritime, river and lake ports;
- deep-water port on the Atlantic coast;
- hospitals and health centres;
- school buildings, training centres, university and higher education sites;
- research centres;
- national, provincial and municipal libraries;
- social housing;
- stations and airports;
- football stadia, sports' infrastructure, playgrounds and leisure parks;
- national and provincial museums;
- cultural and music facilities, etc".

Bilateral and also multilateral associates could play an active part in building up this infrastructure, although, of course, it is evident that the main responsibility lies with the Congolese State. National and also private associations have their place in this undertaking to renovate and reconstruct the infrastructure.

b. *Reform of public companies*

The years 2008 and 2009 were remarkable for their legislative and regulatory output, particularly in the domain of public companies which, up until then, were structured under the framework Law n° 78-002 of 6 January 1978.

This 30-year old text gave way to a series of laws promulgated by the President of the Republic on 7 July 2008 in the context of the reform of public companies because they no longer complied with their initial objectives, namely the provision of goods and services to satisfy the needs of the greatest number of citizens and to contribute to the State's Budget. The following are the laws concerned:

1. Law n° 08/007 of 7 July 2008 covering the general provisions for the transformation of public companies:
   In the context of the general programme for the macroeconomic and sectoral turn around conceived and directed by the government, the objective of this law is to breathe life into a fresh action plan for holding companies and to make their production poten-

151

tial more profitable; to help in reinforcing the competitivity of these companies and the entire national economy.

Hence public companies are thus transformed into commercial companies and governed by common law, or dissolved and shut down.

2. Law n° 08/008 of 7 July 2008 covering the general provisions for the withdrawal of the State from holding companies:

   This withdrawal is justified by the fact that the public companies whose operations are characterised by an inadequate or a lack of financial, economic and social performance need substantial resources that the State cannot offer.

   Moreover, unable to achieve their aims and objectives, they only incur more debts and therefore have become a further drain on public finances.

3. Law n° 08/009 of 7 July 2008 covering the general provisions applicable to public establishments:

   This law is justified by the fact that certain establishments do not perform any lucrative activities but are subjected to the same constraints as bodies operating in the commercial sector.

4. Law n° 08/010 of 7 July 2008 setting out the regulations on the organisation and management of the State's Portfolio:

   This law is designed to ensure that the State's Portfolio has an institutional framework appropriate for the private sector and likely to give a fresh impetus to its management, to promote profitability and to facilitate, if need be, the State's withdrawal.

   It is appropriate to recall that the Congolese State has intervened in the organisation of the economy, not only by adopting legislation but also by taking charge of the running of economic activities. As such, the State has created enterprises, sometimes public sometimes mixed, and has had to manage some substantial sectors like the mines, transport, energy, etc.

The basic reasons for the failure of the 1978 reform of the Portfolio, which prompted that of 2008, may be attributed to:

– the supremacy of public social services over the commercial aspects of providing goods and services;
– abuse of monopoly;

- mismanagement, corruption, misappropriation of public funds, and impunity;
- unjustified and unwarranted appointments of company heads;
- political favouritism, etc.

The 2008 reform basically attempted to discharge the State of responsibility for the commercial sector, which must henceforth be ready to receive private capital and face competition, and be subject to legal common law rulings.

This reform finally targets, as mentioned above, access by private investors to the issued share capital of enterprises converted into commercial companies. And it is exactly with regard to this discharge of the State's responsibility that problems may arise if this discharge does not occur with transparency which only the law on the transfer of public markets can guarantee, as long as a call for public tender is the principal method used.

The Congolese State has the right to expect fresh capital from this reform to finance its economy.

## II. Social dimension

Any political or economic activity only has value when it improves people's standard of living, especially in terms of employment, education, housing, health care and, why not, sport and leisure activities.

From now on a conscious awareness of the social dimension is required. In effect, the strength of those in power is measured henceforth by their capacity to feed their people and to respond adequately to their problems. Otherwise, they are working for nothing and it is no use pretending active engagement, when deceit and inefficiency lie behind it.

Where is DRC in all this?

## A. EMPLOYMENT AND SALARY[270]

The employment situation in DRC is catastrophic. Whilst the country has undergone a strong demographic growth since 1960, the

---

[270] Ministry of Planning, Minimum programme for partnership for transition and revival in DRC, November 2004, abovementioned.

installations producing goods and services have in the main experienced a strong downturn and others have quite simply closed down, which has led to a noticeable reduction in jobs. This situation has been exacerbated on one hand by a lack of a model for accumulating capital and, on the other, in the wake of the measures for Zairianisation mentioned above, from mismanagement, pillage during the tragic times in 1991 and 1993, civil wars and acts of aggression, as well as the burden of taxation.

The development of jobs is hence disproportional to population numbers. A total lack of political willingness to create jobs is apparent.

In effect, around the 1980s, GECAMINES employed 36,000 workers whilst the SNCC and ONATRA had 27,000 and 15,000 employees, respectively.

With the drop in production and the ageing of the production equipment, these large employers in the Republic fired personnel. The jobs lost were not recreated elsewhere. On the contrary, other companies like MIBA, KILO-MOTO, UTEXAFRICA and CHANIMETAL followed in the steps of the other companies three mentioned above. As for the State, the major employer in 1982 and also until quite recently, has greatly reduced the number of its public service workers without providing any replacement jobs, which means a sharp loss of employment in public services.

Another category of companies involves those who have ceased all activity, like BATA, General Motors, BIA, CPA, SOTEXKIN, SIMETAIN, Cotônière, the Unilever Group and its installations, as well as many others.

This situation has worsened unemployment in the university sector, where there is no choice but to turn towards politics, often in a desire for vengeance, and amongst working class youth, at best soon occupied in informal activity, and at worst in criminal activity.

The few lucky ones with a job are happy with remuneration which does not take any account of the standard of living. In this respect, the guaranteed minimum wage (GMW) is currently fixed at 3 USD per day, which is 78 USD per month of 26 working days! Even rarer are those organisations which apply the GMW, starting with the State itself, in spite of the establishment of free trade unions whose proof of efficacy is slow to appear. For certain, the GMW does not apply to the army nor the police force.

In fact, DRC has a unique situation in the world whereby workers may decide to start a strike and end it without its leaders showing any interest in their fate.

In any event, employment is subject to appropriate regulations, allied with just sanctions from the legal system, and is dependent upon the economic and financial health of the country, itself dependent upon good governance. It is highly important because the market, the place where production and consumption meet, is bound up with it. There is no economy without a market.

The State must then encourage the creation of jobs by implementing a policy to stimulate investment, itself a creator of centres of production facilities and hence employment, and to orientate youth towards large agricultural production projects and road maintenance in all provinces.

This last idea is close to that of the National Service conceived by M'Zee Laurent-Désiré Kabila and which was a success[271].

## B. EDUCATIONAL SYSTEM AND SCIENTIFIC RESEARCH

If there is one domain where colonisation has arguments in its favour is that of primary, secondary and university education. In this sphere, the colonial State was supported by religious denominations (Catholic, Protestant, Muslim and Kimbanguist).

In 1972, the nationalisation of universities and higher education denominational institutes was the starting point for disorder in the educational system for higher education. In effect, when shaken by the student protest movements of 1969 and 1971, the main point of contention for the popular protest was when the authority of the day decided to regroup the universities and higher institutes within the National University of Zaïre (UNAZA) so as to keep control in Kinshasa.

---

[271] National Service was the development model instigated by M'Zee Laurent-Désiré Kabila, with a large labour force, where unemployed youth from all provinces were gathered together in Kanyama-Kasese to undertake training for agriculture and even started growing crops. This experience should have spread all over the country but was interrupted by the war of aggression in 1998. The first maize harvest from 15,000 hectares was a success.

Measures by the Zairian State to withdraw schools from the missionaries, around 1974-1975, condemned the national educational system, but the fatal blow occurred when the teachers and operation of the schools were put in charge of pupils' or students' parents.

And yet, when its first university opened in 1956, the University Lovanium in Kinshasa (Catholic); and the two others which followed it, the Official University of Congo in Lubumbashi (public) and the Free University of Congo in Kisangani (Protestant), DRC educated intellectuals had a very good reputation amongst the Congolese, but also amongst the Belgians, the Rwandans, the Burundians, the Cameroonians and other African nationalities who came to study here.

Everybody would agree that the various reforms made to the schools' and academic programmes have contributed to the lowering of teaching standards.

Moreover, it is true to state that there is no quality teaching without scientific research. Now in this domain, the abandonment of research centres erected by the colonial powers is not likely to permit the orderly development of Congolese society.

The research field receives an insignificant portion of the national Budget and, what is more, is not handed over, with the exception, of course, being the scientific personnel's modest remuneration. This disastrous situation explains much about the current stagnation, for the measures taken by the authorities are not part of a well-considered framework, with very precise and comprehensive objectives.

DRC is one of those rare African countries with a research centre for nuclear energy (the CRENK), piloted by national researchers whose level of training leaves nothing to be desired in comparison with their foreign counterparts because they have taken the same courses as they have in the world's best universities. Moreover, the success of the National Institute for Agronomic Study and Research (INERA) should be mentioned. Its efforts were the basis for the acclimatization of the palm oil tree in Malaysia and Indonesia, plus cassava in Nigeria.

However, all is not yet lost because potential does exist. It would suffice to take suitable measures to revive the economy so as to generate the funds necessary to finance the educational and scientific research sectors' needs for infrastructure, a programme and personnel. Taxation could be ring-fenced for specific purposes (parafiscality), to help finance scientific research, the basis of any development.

## C.  HABITAT

Most of the housing in DRC dates from the colonial period due to the involvement of chartered companies, then that of the mining companies (GECAMINES, OKIMO, and MIBA), transport companies (SNCC, ONATRA, AIR ZAIRE) and of the ONL whose activity was taken over by the CNECI, about 1974.

Since then, there have been no more large-scale building programmes. The people have been left to their own devices, with everyone building wherever they want and according to their means, according to their taste.

The town-planning and housing estate laws are relegated into the background, leading to the excessive expansion of cities and increased number of shantytowns where promiscuity reigns supreme. Here, activities of a rural nature are being developed, such as the cultivation of market and other types of gardens.

This state of affairs can change with good policies, which are moving towards an increase in the capacity to produce building materials, using our own natural resources, and by organising marketing outlets.

Whatever the outcome, the housing sector is calling out for suitable legislation and an appropriate banking system. The South African model for credit can usefully be an inspiration for DRC. This involves encouraging the banks to build houses to be sold on long-term credit to people with stable employment.

The habitat of the rural areas must also change. And the best way of finally unblocking the congested towns is to make the villages more viable, with a minimum of social infrastructure.

## D.  HEALTH

The health care system currently established in DRC is far from satisfying the needs of the people because of the dilapidated state of its infrastructure, the lack of medical examination equipment and pharmaceutical products, and also the lack of motivation by the medical and paramedical personnel.

In effect, more than 80% of the installations for receiving patients date from the colonial era. The infrastructure built by the colonials has aged and has not been kept in good condition. This is alarming, especially in the interior of the country where all the teaching hospitals look like real relics from the past.

Since independence, very little effort has been made in this area where it is noticeable that, in spite of everything, a few private health centres have been created, though unfortunately the costs are prohibitively expensive.

The Congolese State loses an enormous amount of money each year by sending patients abroad for treatment that could be provided in the country, where the quality of general practitioners is highly rated in Africa. During the first few years after independence, South Africans came for treatment to the modern GECAMINES' hospitals in Likasi and Lubumbashi. Now the situation is the reverse.

A recrudescence in diseases previously considered eradicated has been observed especially because of poor vaccination coverage for the whole of the territory and little epidemiological monitoring.

There is no well-structured health care insurance system open to the greatest number of people in operation in DRC, fifty years after independence.

The least that can be said is that the health care sector has to be fundamentally reformed, avoiding any window dressing. For the health of the whole nation is today under threat.

The activities of some organisations in the field of health (WHO, UNICEF, UNDP and international and national NGOs) is worthy of attention and to be encouraged since it contributes something, however little, to reducing the devastating effects.

This a sector ready to receive investments as far as both the infrastructure and the health insurance organisations are concerned. To do this, taxation offering exoneration, for example, may be set in place.

The establishment of laboratories and pharmaceutical stocks must also be encouraged to increase access to drugs.

The problem of exorbitant prices must not be ignored. Health insurance bodies will eventually emerge to make up the State's subsides. One government department, like the INSS (national institute for social security) and bodies specially created for this purpose, will emerge to improve medical cover for everybody.

The social dimension is nowadays the Achilles' heel of the country, because it records nothing but regression in all its constituent parts. Yet, the more the social environment is sustained by a high-performance economy, the more it helps support men and women, the main elements for production, in an optimal condition for productivity.

This incomplete review of DRC's potential opportunities shows, if ever this is needed, that this country has enough advantages to make its way out of the current doldrums. It is sufficient to put them into action and put the Congolese people back into work. Added to this, there must be an effort from friendly foreign countries whose response would largely depend on diplomatic activities in acclaiming these advantages beyond national frontiers. An overview of Congolese diplomacy would therefore seem to be indicated.

## CHAPTER II
# Diplomatic and security aspects

It may seem surprising to involve aspects of diplomacy and security when explaining the recurrent crises (economic, political and social) in DRC. However, it has proved obvious that the worsening of these crises is due to a bad conception of diplomacy, which has been more focused on representation than on aspects connected with development.

It is the same for security aspects insufficiently integrated into a worldwide and forward-thinking perspective.

## I. Diplomatic aspects

As soon as DRC obtained international sovereignty on 30 June 1960, it established diplomatic and consular relations with several countries around the world. It is included amongst those countries in Africa with the best representation. It is host in its turn to several diplomatic and consular missions, and also to representative offices of international organisations.

The diplomatic representation of DRC throughout the world is, on one hand, the result of application of an open door policy and, on the other, the diplomacy of prestige and reputation inherited from the Second Republic.

In the recent past, the country had more than 70 representations (embassies, permanent missions and consulates). They currently number 65. Others have been closed either for financial or political reasons, such as in Havana (Cuba), Abu Dhabi (United Arab Emirates), Tehran (Iran), Pyongyang (North Korea), Vienna (Austria) and Mexico City (Mexico). However, it should be noted that North Korea, Cuba and Iran have retained their embassies in Kinshasa.

The Atlantic area has a place of honour in the DRC's diplomatic representation for various reasons: geopolitical and strategic, historical, economic, political and cultural. This representation manifests itself as follows, in the African Zone: Abidjan (Ivory Coast), Accra (Ghana), Abuja (Nigeria), Brazzaville (Congo), Conakry (Guinea), Cotonou (Benin),

Dakar (Senegal), Luanda (Angola), Luena/Consulate (Angola), Libreville (Gabon), Lome (Togo), Monrovia (Liberia), Nouakchott (Mauritania), Pretoria (South Africa), Rabat (Morocco), Yaounde (Cameroon), and Windhoek (Namibia); the European Zone: Berlin (Germany), Brussels (Belgium), The Hague (Netherlands), Lisbon (Portugal), London (United Kingdom), Madrid (Spain), Paris (France) and Stockholm (Sweden); the Americas: Brasilia (Brazil), Buenos Aires (Argentina), Ottawa (Canada), and Washington (United States of America); plus representation at the UN in New York.

Almost half the Congolese diplomatic missions (29) are located in the Atlantic Zone. Some missions are categorised as "Category A": bordering countries (Brazzaville, Luanda), former colonial power (Brussels), Security Council Permanent Member countries (London, Paris, Washington) and privileged partners (Abuja, Pretoria). Embassies in Libreville, Rabat, Brasilia and Ottawa have been raised to the rank of first category

With regard to the increase in its commercial trade with DRC, and its increasing influential presence on the world scene, it is desirable for Brazil to join the list of favoured partners. This demand is also justifiable in respect to the ambitions that the countries around the Atlantic should foster for the promotion of their geographical area.

The diplomatic reform envisaged since 2002 seems to be proceeding towards a regrouping and multiple representation[272]. DRC should only have 38 missions abroad out of the 64 in existence, which is a reduction of 26 posts.

Multiple representation does allow the State to reduce its financial, human and logistical commitments. However, it does have the disadvantage of reducing the country's influence with external powers. Thus, the abovementioned reform can only be temporary, whilst the country waits to acquire the means for a closer and much more proactive diplomacy.

---

[272] The Vienna Convention of 18 April 1961 on diplomatic relations allows multiple diplomatic representation. Article 5, paragraph 1 provides that "the accrediting State, after due notification to the concerned accredited States, may accredit a head of mission or affect a member of the diplomatic staff, according to circumstances, to several states, unless one of the accredited States is expressly opposed to it".

Diplomacy is also a reflection of the country's image towards the exterior. The current state of dilapidation of the infrastructure of our embassies and the impoverishment of the diplomatic personal must cease as quickly as possible.

## II. Security aspects

Security aspects are taken into consideration in the relations between DRC and the countries around the Atlantic.

## A. RELATIONS WITH REPUBLIC OF CONGO (BRAZZAVILLE)

Relations with the Republic of the Congo have been normalised since the 1970s after the conclusion of the Manifest of 16 June 1970 and the Franceville Agreement of 18 August 1972, thanks to some fiery mediation by President Omar Bongo Ondiba of Gabon. As a result of this process, both countries have signed several agreements of a commercial, scientific, technical and cultural nature[273].

However, two major problems remain: the management of the influx of immigrants and the security of the common section of the River Congo. Regular discussions between the governments of both countries allow the crises to be resolved. A non-aggression pact, signed in Brazzaville on 29 December 1998, links the two Congos. Article 2 of the pact is quite eloquent when it states as follows: "In the terms of this Agreement, the Pact of non-aggression is understood as: the commitment of the parties not to have recourse in their reciprocal relations to threats or the employment of force, or to aggression against the territorial integrity or independence of the other party. The parties thus undertake not to commit, encourage or support any acts of hostility or aggression against the territorial integrity or independence of the other party."

---

[273] MAVUNGU, J.-P., *Politique étrangère de la République Démocratique du Congo*, Course notes, Law Faculty of the University of Kinshasa, second year of degree course, 2008-2009, unpublished.

## B. RELATIONS WITH REPUBLIC OF ANGOLA

DRC and Angola share a common border over 2,000 km in length. As in Congo Brazzaville, several ethnic groups and tribes (Lunda, Kongo, Luba, Tshokwe, etc.) straddle the two countries. These factors require the establishment and consolidation of friendly relations.

Angola flew to the rescue of DRC, alongside Namibia and Zimbabwe, during the war of aggression on 2 August 1998.

However, two thorny issues need to be handled impartially: the management of the cross-border movement of people and the demarcation of land and maritime borders.

### 1. Cross-border movements of people

The influx of migrants of past decades started with the struggles by Angola for independence from Portugal. DRC gave shelter to many Angolans, notably to people from the Kongo ethnic group, located along the Atlantic coastline.

After Angola's independence, a massive influx of young people from several African countries, including Congo, was observed.

### 2. The demarcation of borders

A maritime dispute exists, based on control of the petroleum deposits on the continental shelf and the fish resources in territorial waters, which will have to be settled by agreement between the two countries. Moreover, the existence of elements from the Angolan army, in several places in DRC, particularly in Kahemba (Bandundu) and in Bas-Fleuve (the Lower-Congo), have been discovered.

A parliamentary mission had been dispatched to Luanda in 2007, at the height of the border conflict on the Kahemba issue, and the National Assembly had recommended the DRC government to favour diplomacy and bilateral negotiations to settle any possible dispute between Angola and our country. Since then, both parties have begun negotiations with assistance from the former colonial powers (Belgium and Portugal)[274]

---

[274] See DRC National Assembly, *Rapport de la Commission d'enquête parlementaire*, Kinshasa, 2008.

The settlement on friendly terms of these boundary issues or the influx of immigrants is dictated by the fact that the two countries are longstanding allies and because of the role played by Angola alongside DRC during the last wars of aggression.

At regional level, DRC has agreed to the mechanisms for collective security established by the ECCAS, SADC and the International Conference on the Great Lakes Region[275].

## C. MILITARY COOPERATION WITH COUNTRIES AROUND THE ATLANTIC

Outside the African continent, and for several years, DRC has maintained military cooperation with several countries from the North Atlantic, principally Belgium, France and the United States of America.

Belgium has participated in the training of brigades incorporated in the FARDC (the Armed Forces of DRC), the strengthening of the military engineering capacity and the training of elite troops (rapid intervention force, based in Kindu, in the province of Maniema).

Military cooperation with France was more dynamic under the Second Republic[276]. The failings observed in the country's defence system during the two Shaba wars led France to assist with the restructuring of the Zairian Armed Forces. The general Agreement on technical and military cooperation between the French and Zairian Republics, signed in Kinshasa on 22 May 1974, included three components: assistance to personnel through the dispatch of military advisors, the instruction of trainee soldiers in France and logistical assistance.

Military cooperation between the two countries produced significant results, in particular: the supply of Mirage V jets to Zaire and armoured car squads, the training and supervision of the 311th para-

---

[275]  Cf. The non-aggression Pact signed in Yaounde on 8 July 1996 by the ECCAS Member States; the mutual assistance Pact between the ECCAS Member States signed in Malabo on 24 February 2000 with respect to crisis management and threats of crisis; the SADC Protocol for cooperation in political, defence and security matters, amended in Kinshasa on 8 September 2009; the Pact on the security, stability and development in the Great Lakes region, signed in Nairobi on 15 December 2006.

[276]  See in particular CHAIGNEAU, P., *La politique militaire de la France en Afrique*, Paris, CHEAM, 1984; BALMOND, L. (ed.), *Les intererventions militaries françaises en Afrique*, Paris, Pedone, 1998.

chute brigade and the armoured division at Mbanza-Ngungu in the province of Lower-Congo (EFATBL – Armoured Car Training School), maintenance of Alouette helicopters and Mirage jets.

France is the military power that has intervened most in DRC[277]. The Agreement on military assistance, suspended since November 1992, needs to be revised and updated.

Under the auspices of the Common Security and Defence Policy (CSDP), the European Union Council sent two security missions on behalf of DRC[278]:

– A mission by the European Union Police (EUPOL-Kinshasa), to train and equip a specialist police unit: the Unity of Integrated Police (UPI), with a budget of 10 million euros. The UPI was responsible for ensuring the protection of the State's institutions and to strengthen the internal security operation to guarantee that elections were fair;
– A mission to advise and assist with reform of the security sector in the DRC (EUSEC DRC), in order to help with a successful integration of the army.

Until recent times, Africa was given little consideration in the foreign policy of the United States of America; traditional priorities were given to Europe, Latin America, the Middle East and Asia. Africa was considered as a region of secondary importance. The Americans preferred to leave responsibility for security and stability on the African continent with the former colonial powers[279].

Thanks to AGOA (the African Growth and Opportunity Act) and US-AFRICOM (the US Military Command for Africa) special attention has been paid to a few countries considered as poles for growth and

---

[277] 1977: Shaba I (logistical assistance); 1978: Shaba II (engagement of the foreign 2nd parachute regiment): 1992: operation "Baumier" (to protect and evacuate French residents); 1995: operation "Turquoise" in Rwanda (logistical bases in Zaire); 2003: operation "Artemis" in the Ituri district of the Eastern Province (European force under French command).

[278] Cf. MAVUNGU, J.-P., "Le rôle de l'Union européenne dans le processus ...", *op. cit.*, p. 231.

[279] Cf. KASPI, A., "La politique africain des Etats-Unis", in *L'Afrique noire depuis la Conférence de Berlin*, Paris, CHEAM (Centre des Hautes Études sur l'Afrique), 1985, p. 163.

with a strategic interest: South Africa, Angola, Nigeria, DRC, Uganda, etc.

President Barack OBAMA has inaugurated a new era in relations between the United States and Africa, based on partnership: "Before, the United States worked for Africa. Now we want to work with Africa (...). This partnership with Africa will be based on mutual responsibility and respect. This mutual responsibility must be the basis for our partnership and involve the four following areas: democracy, economic opportunities, health and the peaceful settlement of conflicts. We must support powerful and lasting democracies."[280].

Under the auspices of AFRICOM, in Kinshasa on 19 June 2009, the United States and DRC signed a military cooperation agreement, based on the training of the rapid intervention force of the FARDC[281].

With respect to peace and security, the countries bordering the Atlantic may combine their efforts to strengthen the capacities of African armies (training, equipment, exchange of information, etc.) to warn of threats, to help with conflict settlement, to combat terrorism, drug trafficking, money laundering, the traffic in people, clandestine immigration, the illegal trade in arms and the proliferation of nuclear weapons, etc.

When it is known that bases for international terrorism in Africa are to be found in southern Algeria, northern Mali, Sudan and in Somalia and that terrorists have already struck against countries like Kenya and Tanzania, close to DRC, the compulsion to stabilise the country is understandable, so that it may become a bastion for stability and the anti-terrorist struggle in Sub-Saharan Africa

As a country at the cross-road of several African regions, DRC has a right to play an active part in tricontinental cooperation to stamp out these scourges.

---

[280]  Speech given in Accra (Ghana), July 2009, cf. *Le Potentiel* n° 4686 of 29 July 2009, p. 2.
[281]  Cf. Agence congolaise de Presse, via meddiacongo.net, 22 June 2009.

# Partial conclusion – Part Two

As can be observed, DRC possesses the assets which should have enabled its economic and social objectives to take off. The main reason for the failure to take advantage of these opportunities lies with bad governance at both political and economic levels.

As a prerequisite for economic development, good governance is in fact the sound and transparent management of economic, financial, human and natural resources, with a heightened sense of responsibility, without corruption, and involving justice, steadfastness and discipline. This means developing a culture of results.

Hence good governance is in some ways like a discipline in which an experienced climber, a monitor, invites the ordinary climbers to respect the markers that he has placed along the way. This is the kind of exercise that Africans in general and the Congolese in particular will be bound to perform to restructure their State and improve their living conditions. It is urgent to put the principles of good governance into practice in the interests of the community.

This is not impossible provided that the political will is duly confirmed and commitments respected.

PART THREE

# REASONS TO EXPECT A PROSPEROUS AND POWERFUL FUTURE CONGO

# Introduction

To shape the future, a revaluation must be made, strategies reconsidered, renouncing those which have demonstrated their limitations and putting into practice a fresh vision for the management of the resources available, Above and beyond the volition to perform better, there must be a commitment to improvement.

This part includes an analysis of the perspectives in the short and medium terms (Chapter I) and will explain our confidence in a better future for Congo (Chapter II).

CHAPTER I

# Short- and long-term perspectives

What is the future of transatlantic relationships and what role can DRC play in them?

To reply optimistically to these questions, it is critical to consider two approaches:

- on one hand, to put in place an institutional mechanism likely to formalise transatlantic relationships;
- on the other, to make DRC a land of hope for the world in general and for the transatlantic zone in particular.

## I. Future of transatlantic relationships: need for an institutional mechanism

After the Cold War period and in light of current issues, it seems as if the creation of structures or a mechanism for cooperation like NATO or the Union for the Mediterranean would be collectively and individually beneficial for the countries alongside the Atlantic.

The establishment of a CTA, *Conférence Tricontinental Atlantique* (or Tricontinental Atlantic Conference) would enable a better identification of the areas for cooperation and ensure a better coordination for them. The CTA could integrate elements such as: a Conference of Heads of State and Government, a Ministerial Conference, a Technical Secretariat and *ad hoc* Commissions.

The creation of the CTA to encompass the entire tricontinental Atlantic zone is justified with regard to the issues raised by Dorval BRUNELLE and Christian DEBLOCK, when they declare with regard to the North American Free Trade Agreement (NAFTA): "Ten years after it came into force on 1 January 1994, the North American Free Trade Agreement is now at a cross-roads. Considered as a model commercial agreement, sufficiently flexible to adapt itself to the demands of globalisation and robust enough to make access easier to later forms of integration, NAFTA has introduced new dynamics into the integrating and institutional plan. Yet, the plan seems well and truly lacking at the current moment: those who were favourable to it fear that it will no longer be able to face new challenges and those hostile to it reproach it for exacerbating the economic, social and political asymmetry inside the North American region. The basic question at the moment is: must we stay with it or must we envisage something else? "[282].

Transatlantic cooperation involves the following priority domains:

- peace, defence and security;
- fight against terrorism and drug trafficking;
- economy and trade;
- agriculture;
- environment;
- energy;
- technology transfer;
- culture;
- new communication and information technologies;
- management of movements of immigrants;
- fair trade development.

Considering the spread of terrorism in Africa, with incursions by al-Qaida into the north, north-west and east of the continent, as well as the transnational criminal activities linked to the trafficking of drugs and light arms, the subject matter is not short on interest.

Given the inequality of development between the Northern and Southern Hemispheres of the Atlantic Zone, an inequality often blamed on the absence of a mechanism for solidarity between the two hemispheres, the CTA would provide a framework for the establishment of innovative regulatory policies, and would operate in the image of NATO which, at the time it was created, had placed the Western European countries under the protective wing of the United States, with the objective of minimising the possible threats of military invasion from the Communist Bloc.

Due to common policies marked by their solidarity, and supported by a conscientious internal administration in every State, these coun-

---

[282] BRUNELLE D., and DEBLOCK, C., L'ALENA, *Le libre-échange en défaut*, Montreal, Fides, Coll. Points chauds, 2004.

tries closed the gap, and most of them hoisted themselves up to the peak, to figure amongst the richest nations on earth.

The situation of our countries in the Southern Hemisphere of the Atlantic Zone (Latin America and Africa), weakened by a long period of calamitous public administration (dictatorships, armed conflicts bad governance, misappropriation by a tiny minority of all the national wealth, etc.) resembles that of countries in Western Europe at the end of the Second World War.

The South Atlantic countries would not come empty-handed to this alliance especially when some like Brazil, Mexico, Nigeria, South Africa, Angola and DRC have been blessed with immense potential resources.

## II. DRC: land of hope for humanity

Hence, judging from what emerges from preceding chapters, it is no exaggeration to claim that with its human resources and its enormous potential opportunities above and below ground, in the water and the forests, DRC in time of peace is an opportunity for the transatlantic area which means that it may be able to bring some solutions to the various crises occurring in the area.

In contrast, abandoned to conflicts that are sometimes not of its own making, such as those currently occurring in its Eastern territory, this country is becoming an abyss dragging everyone towards the bottom, including the Atlantic Region.

The demonstration of its capacity to find responses to these crises is an exercise which is worth exploring.

## A. HUMAN RESOURCES

It is obvious that people, as perceived by their capacity to create and consume wealth, are the primary resource of any nation.

For its part, DRC is a young nation, with an independent existence for scarcely 50 years, which has a university tradition a little bit older than itself (the first university opened in 1956, although the country did not become independent until 1960).

Nowadays, this great country includes senior managers, men and women, educated in almost all disciplines of science, technology, culture and the arts. A number of these managers have received high-level education in the prestigious universities of both the North and the South.

Congolese scientists offer their services to the country and to the entire world. They are university professors, engineers, doctors, technicians, jurists, political scientists, historians and specialists in various fields, including the new technologies.

In this light, DRC is usefully equipped for collaboration with the countries of the Atlantic Region in various sectors, from conception to the production of goods and services.

With its population of nearly 70 million inhabitants, DRC is one of the most important markets in Africa and particularly along the Atlantic shoreline. The mobile phone companies operating in Kinshasa would not disagree.

In this respect, the drawback is the population's low level of income, although this is a factor likely to be corrected with time and effort.

The personal commitment that may be made to the Nation is to rise to the major challenge of the task to put human beings, the citizens, at the heart of any policy being conducted. In fact, economic development cannot be an end in itself; it must help improve people's living standards. If they do not see any progress achieved in terms of improvement to their day-to-day wellbeing, any progress is nothing but an illusion.

And because the development of a country can only be based upon the work and sacrifices of its people, it is important for the elite to prepare the body of workers to fully commit themselves to the fight against poverty and ignorance.

To achieve this, the State must, in the immediate term, invest in the priority sectors which are health, education and agriculture. For it cannot be said often enough, "the most important resource in any country is its people and, if a large part of its inhabitants cannot put their own potential to work – because they do not have access to education, or because for their whole life they endure the effects of the malnutrition suffered during childhood –, nor can the country allow its own potential to materialise"[283].

Afar from this argument linked to human resources, DRC can respond to many specific crises.

## B. WORLD FOOD CRISIS

DRC, in common with a good many developing countries, is today suffering from a substantial shortage of food.

Yet its surface area and its transverse situation in relation to the Equator give it a climate, flora and rainfall suitable for agriculture and animal farming.

According to FAO statistics[284], if well exploited, Congolese arable land could feed more than 2 billion individuals, which is a third of humanity, and twice the current population of Africa. Its rivers, tributaries and lakes are very rich in fish which, in some cases, as in Lake Tanganyika, are dying of old age. To combat its food shortage the country can also rely upon its grasslands and mountains which are suitable for animal rearing and high altitude crops.

But to achieve this both noble and humanitarian objective, the involvement of players, private and public from the transatlantic region, is more than necessary.

Before solving the world food crisis, we have to feed our own population. As demonstrated above, the Brazilian model is suited to the country's situation. M'Zee Laurent Désiré Kabila's National Service scheme, together with a focus on agriculture in the provinces, are likely to give agricultural production the necessary impetus and respond to the challenges of the food crisis.

---

[283] STIGLITZ, J., Nobel prize for economics, *Un autre monde, contre le fanatisme du marché*, Paris, Fayard, 2006, in the French translation.

[284] Cf. www.worldbank.org; www.adicie.com/archives, *L'intégration des statistiques agricoles et rurales dans l'étude des filières des principales cultures vivrières en République Démocratique du Congo*, 20th session of the commission for agricultural statistics for Africa, held in Algiers from 10 to 23 December 2007.

## C. ENERGY CRISIS

The world is now suffering an energy crisis which is worsening from year to year, in proportion to the increased needs of the world's population which are increasing at an accelerated pace, especially in the majority of third world countries. Recourse to hydrocarbons, coal and nuclear energy has already shown its limitations because of the harmful effect on the environment in terms of pollution and risks of catastrophies able to affect populations (case of Tchernobyl), but also due to the depleting reserves of all these deposits.

It is true that new projects are being developed for the production of biofuels and wind turbines. If the latter has its limitations in locating appropriate sites, as far as the production of biofuels is concerned, arable land must not be used for this to the detriment of food production.

DRC offers vast hydroelectric potential opportunities, estimated, as may be recalled, at 100,000 MW, which is 13 % of the worldwide hydroelectric potential.

When the Inga IV project at the Inga Dam is completed, this alone could supply clean, renewable and non-polluting electricity, to several African countries and even to countries in Southern Europe. Far and beyond the African continent, the Inga site could be considered as a tricontinental cooperation project.

In addition, the methane gas at Lake Kivu is an important energy source for the domestic and especially industrial needs of a large part of Eastern Africa, with reserves estimated at 65 billion Nm$^3$. In actual fact and as mentioned earlier, this lake is recharged with gas at a rate of 250 million Nm$^3$ each year. This rate has increased to 350 million Nm$^3$ annually over the past 15 years, to the extent that it constitutes a potential danger to the people living nearby if this gas continues to accumulate at the same pace.

Besides these sources of "clean energy", DRC has reserves of petroleum estimated at more than 1.3 billion barrels.

## D. WATER CRISIS

Water will become, if it is not already, the key factor in the survival of many countries in Africa and worldwide since access to drinking water and water for agriculture is, at this moment, a strategic matter.

The water potential in DRC, which accounts for 53% of freshwater reserves in Africa, thus becomes a vital matter for all the people living below the Sahara and above the Kalahari.

Water is needed for men and animals to survive, for the development of industry, transport systems and agriculture.

With the River Congo, its tributaries, other rivers, streams and natural springs, its lakes at the eastern border and also inside its territory, DRC represents a vast reserve of freshwater. To put it quite simply, it is Africa's water storage tower.

This sector provides opportunities for cooperation for a rational exploitation to meet the needs of the desert regions in Africa. DRC has some strong arguments to make in this particular domain.

## E. GLOBAL WARMING

Global warming has become one of the major issues since the end of the last century.

The proliferation of world conferences on this subject (Rio de Janeiro, Kyoto and recently Copenhagen) well illustrate the importance of the issue of global warming which seriously threatens Planet Earth, because of the greenhouse gas emissions polluting our atmosphere.

DRC, through its vast forest, has an important contribution to make to resolve this problem. Its 145 million hectares of tropical forests (which is, as may be recalled, two-thirds of the forest surface in the Congo Basin and the second largest mass of tropical forest in the world) uncover an amazing diversity of wealth, species of forest trees, flora and fauna, fish stocks, etc.

If DRC does, to any significant extent, take advantage of the resource that cut and exported wood represent in terms of foreign currency, it is not, however, desirable that this activity should become more extensive and so deprive the world of one of its lungs, to which the Congo Basin has been compared. Therefore, the future management of the Congolese forest will have to take account of the implications for the planet. This would justify adequate compensation for the loss in earnings that meeting this requirement would create.

But the existence of this potential is not enough. To fully play the role it has been given to solve the challenges, the country still has to become organised and obtain the status which would enable it to be recognised and to make itself respected in the chorus of nations.

# CHAPTER II

# Faith in a better future for DRC

Apart from some persistent and wearisome problems, there must be belief in the future of DRC. This belief is based on specific action plans and on the means employed to carry them out.

## I. Action plans to be implemented

These action plans involve:

– the restructuring of the State;
– establishment of good governance;
– improvement in the living conditions of the population;
– pursuit of complete and sustainable development;
– establishment of a different and accountable leadership.

## A. RESTRUCTURING THE STATE

Bad management of all things public, the wars and the rebellions that have shaken DRC, and which are still going on now, have disconnected the State from its sovereign responsibilities. They must be totally re-established to restore peace and security in the country, conditions *sine quae non* for any development.

Peace and security are conducive to reconstruction, whilst war and rebellions are destructive, costly and ruinous.

To restructure the State means restoring the country's administration, justice system, army, police, security forces and diplomacy which must be national and republican.

The large State departments must be cured of the ills that they have endured and which are essentially corruption, misappropriation, tribalism, favouritism, nepotism, demotivation and under-equipment.

These ills must be combated by making the courts truly independent, to fight against corruption and misappropriation of public funds, and to reorganise entrance to the civil service, notably by setting examinations for admission, to respect rules of promotion and to restore top-level schools for the civil service. Careers must be supervised individually and not collectively from recruitment to retirement.

Moreover, respect for rights and individual and collective freedoms play a part in strengthening the State, which must make itself more secure by reaffirming and carrying out the principles of neighbourly relations and a worldwide open door policy, in accordance with rules of international law. During the State's restructuring phase, diplomacy must be for development and performed by career diplomats.

The ending of impunity must not be limited to merely talking about it, if not, the strong have immunity and the weak are sacrificed.

We would stress, nevertheless, that in the quest to restructure the State, Congo is ahead of some other African States, by taking responsibility for its currency, a prelude to the economic independence sought by many African countries.

In 1967, the then president, Joseph Désiré Mobutu Sese Seko, endowed DRC with its own currency, the Zaire. At its launch, 1 Z equalled 2 USD.

Later, in his turn, M'Zee Laurent Désiré Kabila, after he took power in 1997, launched a new currency, the Congolese franc, which continues to be the country's legal tender.

Both initiatives are rare in Black Africa where the currency of many countries is supported by strong western currencies.

This was one way for Congo to assert its sovereignty. It is true that the Congolese franc, like any other money, is only the reflection of the health of our economy, and is sick at the moment, "When the country is doing badly, its money can do nothing else but do badly too. We need to have a strong currency for our country's image. Currency is a symbol, it is also a barometer for the country's economy, and we need a strong currency – the equal of the Congolese franc."[285]

A State cannot be strong, however, without respecting good governance.

---

[285] MASANGU MULUNGO, J.C., *Pourquoi je crois au progrès de l'Afrique*, Paris, Prestige Communication, 2020, p. 69.

## B.  GOOD GOVERNANCE

Modern States are today administered to respect standards which include a conventional management of public assets and finances, and the transparency of the public administration through the principles of regular evaluation, control by the people through its representatives, and by the separation of powers.

The weak point in the conduct of affairs of State in Africa is still the lack of control over State administration. Parliaments are restricted to one single duty, to legislate, although all constitutions also give them the duty to control governments. Unfortunately, the latter duty often clashes with the will of those in power. And yet, power should be bound by law and not the law by force.

As the task of controlling the administration is often neglected in Africa, those who are being administered could hardly expect any positive outcome from the activities of the administrators.

## C.  IMPROVEMENT IN LIVING CONDITIONS OF THE POPULATION

Peoples' living conditions are bound up with their access to social and other services to ensure their wellbeing; these are essentially:

– food, water and electricity;
– education;
– health care;
– housing or habitat;
– social justice for everyone.

With its arable land, its abundance of fresh water, its vast forests and its hydroelectric potential, Congo, with a clear vision and well defined objectives, should reduce if not solve its problems of access to food, drinking water and electricity.

Unfortunately this is not now happening. Rates for water and electricity distribution are amongst the lowest in Africa whilst undernourishment affects people in several parts of the country. In reality, according to some statistics[286], over 70 % of the Congolese live on less than one dollar per day!

---

[286]  Indicators on gender, poverty and the environment in African countries, African Development Bank, Statistics Division, 2004.

In addition, the primary wealth of any nation can be judged today by the number of its intellectuals. On this issue, DRC must redesign its obsolete educational system, make an inventory of its senior managers and employ them wisely and for good use.

How can you think about developing Congo without reforming the university, the university professor, researcher, the academic, teacher, in short, education and, generally speaking, all the players in it?

People also need access to appropriate health care. The deterioration in the health infrastructure, obsolescence and the lack of equipment are a major obstacle to the establishment of a health system worthy of the name, although DRC does not lack qualified personnel. At least 2000 Congolese doctors practise in South Africa and there are others in the rest of southern Africa and throughout the world. As a first step, the existing infrastructure should be renovated and re-equipped, before envisaging any expansion.

On independence, DRC inherited one of the most effective health infrastructures in Africa. At that time, in each territory (144 in all), in each town (more than forty), there was at least one large hospital and one reference clinic, to the point where South Africans, just to mention one example, came to be treated in the hospitals of Elisabethville, now Lubumbashi, and Jadotville, currently Likasi.

Nowadays, through lack of maintenance and investment in line with demographic and technological expansion and because of inadequate health policies, this trend has been reversed; all the sick Congolese, of course those who are well off, make their way to South Africa, whilst the poor are left to their sorry fate.

For the wellbeing of its people, the Congolese elite also have a duty to reflect upon the type of environment that links comfort with the costs of making it possible for the majority. In this area, recourse can be had to readily available local material, which would to a large extent solve the problem of maintenance. Special emphasis should be given to improving the rural environment, to make villages really viable places, so as to help combat the rural exodus.

Not wishing to go back as far as the colonial era, a short outline of the recent history of the environment and housing can throw a better light upon our meaning.

When the country became independent, public intervention in the field of urban planning was practically inexistent. Nevertheless, a few public institutions as well as some private initiatives made some positive progress. This was the case in 1965 when the *Office National du Logement* (ONL) (or national housing office), which had succeeded the *Office des Cités Africaines* (OCA) (or office for African housing projects) in order to carry on the tasks of the former as well as those of the Advance Funds. The Congolese will remember the ONL, dissolved in 1987, for its poor performance and achievements in comparison with those of the two bodies that it had replaced[287].

Also noteworthy is the creation in 1971 of the *Caisse Nationale d'Épargne et de Crédit Immobilier* (CNECI) (or national savings and mortgage bank). This public body was designed on the model of the OCA, with a special feature whereby it obtained its resources from private savings and granted medium- and long-term loans to build, acquire or renovate modest housing. Unfortunately, the CNECI relied more on the construction and operation of "turnkey" properties. Hence, it did not last more than the space of four years, and its results to say the least were mixed[288].

Other initiatives are now worth mentioning. This is the case with *"Habitat pour l'Humanité"* (or the environment for humanity). Thanks to support from the American Protestant churches, this non-governmental organisation built more than 2000 homes in DRC between 1974 and 1999. The bulk of its activities are concentrated in the Equator Province.

For its part, the *Logément Économique* (LOGEC) (or Economic Housing) has benefited since its creation from resources from two parastatal companies, the *Société Nationale d'Electricité* (SNEL) (or national electric company) and the *Régie de Distribution, des Eaux* (REGIDESO) (or Water Distribution Company). LOGEC was the main contributor to the construction of the "Cite Mama Mobutu", completed in 1988.

---

[287] The OCA's work mainly consisted in low-cost construction of a large number of houses made of long-lasting material, but also work on infrastructure and collective equipment in the new neighbourhoods.

[288] The four years' existence of the CNECI (1971-1975) in the end only enabled the building of 845 homes, only 800 houses of the 1000 predicted for the "Cité Salongo" in the Lemba district.

Currently, there is no single State body responsible for building social or any other kind of housing. Faced with the thorny problem of housing, as very many Congolese households are, and weary of waiting for solutions promised decades ago, each person has become resolved to make his/her own arrangements; shanties and flimsy homes made from recycled material (old sheet metal and other materials used in the manufacture of bottle tops, multiplex sheets, tree bark, metal building strips, tarred cardboard, tarpaulins, straightened barrels, cardboard packaging, etc., with corrugated iron used most often as a roof). This is the "slum creation" process which we are witnessing not only in the capital but also in all the country's urban centres[289].

Thus, to ensure food, water, electricity, education health care and housing, it is the State's job to achieve the social and collective justice that will enable Congolese society to achieve a balanced development and to make each person play a part in the collective effort, whilst guaranteeing each citizen a just reward. A society built on this foundation is equipped with the means and with solidarity to face up to the challenges which arise on the way towards development.

But apart from this vision in the short- and medium-term, we are convinced that our country, as we have previously tried to demonstrate, possesses the means and resources to determine and implement the objectives of a complete and long-lasting development.

## D.  COMPLETE AND LONG-LASTING DEVELOPMENT

The requirement for complete and long-lasting development will notably include the revival of production, the protection and the rational management of the environment, as well as the construction of infrastructure and recourse to new technologies.

There is hardly any point in repeating that a country's economy depends upon its production of goods and services.

DRC has greatly regressed in this area, since its mining industry (GÉCAMINES, OKIMO, MIBA SOMINKI) is practically at a standstill.

---

[289]  KANENE, M., *Assainissements des sites inondables à Kinshasa, cite des pêcheurs à Kingabwa,* PNUD/CNUEH-Habitat, Kinshasa, 2001.

186

The revival of mining activity requires the mobilisation of significant financial means. According to estimates made by the government's experts, an envelope of more or less eight billion American dollars would be necessary to revive production of copper, cobalt, diamonds and gold.

Besides, agriculture and animal farming are promising sectors which will not create too many problems to revive them.

As has been mentioned previously, the development of the mining, manufacturing and agro-food industry can only be conceived as part of a plan which incorporates features linked to the protection of investments.

## E. ESTABLISHMENT OF A DIFFERENT AND RESPONSIBLE LEADERSHIP

This new leadership should be installed after all the following procedures have been heeded:

a) **To take account of objective criteria** in the appointment and promotion of those leaders called upon to direct the large State structures and the Portfolio companies. These criteria should be based on ethical and moral considerations plus technical competence.

b) **To accept the principle of change**, with a new way of managing public assets. It is unacceptable to see DRC stagnate in the midst of an endemic crisis of governance and leadership with dramatic consequences. Our country is not a model for "good governance"; it can even be described as "bad" or with a "lack of governance" leading to the decline of the State. This situation puts the people at the mercy of local and foreign opportunists of any kind, such as warlords or traffickers, in cahoots with the masters of international terrorism and organised crime. The country has a bad reputation which must be brought to an end.

To allow this situation to carry on is to condemn 70 million Congolese and seriously mortgage international peace and security. Hence we have to put everything in order to restore legitimate and responsible leadership to our country and its people, in the context of a project for the development of society.

In fact, modern States are administered nowadays in respect of the standards which are included in any conventional management of assets and public finance, together with transparency in public administration, guaranteed by principles of periodic audit, of control by the people via its representatives and the separation of power. Accounting procedures allow just such an audit to be carried out. This will be our battle cry in the fight against the deterioration in public finances.

c) **To reinforce the conciliatory operation of public institutions** in order to make them more likely to meet the expectations of the people by improving living conditions and the establishment of an economy to serve the citizen.

In fact, the living conditions of any person are linked to access to social and welfare services which are in the main: food, water, electricity, education, health care, housing or environment, social and collective justice, plus leisure.

d) **To promote the status of women** in order to give deserving women access to all political and public functions, without exception, and thus ensure respect of the principle of equality of men and women as asserted in the Constitution.

e) **To encourage youth education** and professional training to meet the challenges of sustainable, complete and total development, which requires the mobilisation and implication of young people. In fact, we intend to promote a consistent policy to create employment for young people who leave professional schools, universities and higher educational institutes but also for the very many people condemned to unemployment due to the fact that public policies have led to recurrent economic crises in our country, well before the current international financial crisis. Such an objective will be pursued by means of infrastructure construction and the application of a policy of credit to support potentially profitable development projects in high growth sectors such as agro-industry, animal farming, and hotels, sectors which should contribute to the creation of wealth.

A policy for a decent salary based on a GMW to be negotiated and imposed on companies, will be courageously and enthusiastically carried out, in order to improve the living conditions of the working classes as much as for the protection of the labour force. In this situation, it will be possible to achieve a sustainable, complete and integrated development for DRC.

## II. Resources to be promoted for a rational and far-sighted exploitation, in association with worldwide investors

It is important to recall that for more than a century the Congolese mining basin has experienced large-scale exploitation with financial assistance from large chartered companies who supported the expansion activities of King Leopold II in building his Independent Congo State, and later on Belgium, as a colonial power. Since this time, the country has always been open to the world and is ready to welcome investments from all those interested in making use of its resources. Following the failure of the economic policies established after the country's independence, it is even more urgent to reconsider the strategy. In this situation, the policy for partnerships through active contractual agreements is appropriate, but it does seem to favour the interests of the public players more than the State's. The main point is to avoid signing one-sided contracts with these partners. Some of these have been the subject of discussions and incited unfavourable comments.

Hence, these riches that should have led to complete development seem to be the source of misfortune or curses on the country. This ought not to be a source of pride, but completely the opposite, and it is time to call the elite and the ruling class to account. As George SOROS writes in his work entitled *L'âge de la faillibilité*, "developing countries who are rich in natural resources tend to be as poor as those countries who are less well endowed; what does distinguish them is that they usually have more repressive and corrupt governments and that they are often devastated by armed conflict. This situation ended up by being called 'the curse of resources'."[290]

If Brazil has succeeded in less than ten years in becoming powerful and autonomous, in being ranked among emerging countries, Congo, with all its advantages and opportunities, can do the same. Nothing

---

[290] SOROS, G., quoted by BAKANDEJA wa MPUNGU, G., *Droit minier et des hydro-carbures ...*, *op. cit.*

is impossible for the Congolese. The Atlantic provides an area for commercial trade between the countries around it, but also between them and the rest of the world.

The current bridge-building between Brazil and DRC, made concrete by diplomatic and commercial ties, should be congratulated as it could be a stimulus for the Congolese to make them believe in the economic take-off of their country.

Commercial ties between DRC and Brazil have been experiencing remarkable growth for some years. The bilateral trade volume, although still very weak, has increased from 17 million USD in 2005 to 210 million in 2007, which is a rise of 1,235 % in two years. Several Brazilian companies are established in DRC: Vale (in the mining sector in Katanga), HRT-Petroleum (evaluation of petroleum deposits in the Congolese Central Basin), Commercial Transport Agency (importation of machines and equipment for the mining industry), Adex Sprl (diamond trade), etc. Congolese exports to Brazil basically include mining products and oil.

In its turn, and as mentioned previously, DRC imports various products from Brazil, such as poultry (33.6 %), cereals (21.5 %), sugar and confectionery products (14.8 %), cattle (5.4 %) and plastics (3.6 %). The country may profit from these commercial ties to obtain a technology transfer which should enable it to achieve local production in order to be self-sufficient in food.

Another sector where DRC ought to draw inspiration from Brazil's experience is that of its ability to contribute toward the fight against global warming.

In fact, both countries possess the two largest equatorial forests and play a large part in the elimination of greenhouse gases. But now, only Brazil, through the right policies and active diplomacy, managed to play its cards right in the matter of global warming and in defence of biodiversity, by obtaining financial compensation from those countries polluting the planet.

It is up to DRC to set its pitch to obtain compensation proportional to its contribution and the restrictions imposed on its population in the matter of environmental protection.

Moreover, it is urgent for DRC to diversify its commercial relations with other countries in the American Atlantic area to increase its influence.

# Partial conclusions – Part Three

Evidently, the obstacles to economic development are enormous for a country after a civil war, as is the case with DRC. Can this country hope to experience real long-term growth and economic development? We believe it can. In reality, since the ending of a war which was imposed on the country, it is progressively restructuring and has taken steps towards democratisation and hence development. It started timidly with a return to the international scene, notably by means of economic and legal integration within the African continent.

Its population, estimated at approximately 70 million people, is commercially one of the most dynamic, even though this dynamism does not yet profit the State because of the informal nature of the economy. DRC must create a new class of entrepreneurs. They should be innovative in building their wealth and participate in market capitalism instead of participating in the current informal economy and they should no longer want to invest their capital outside the country.

In reality, when the black economy assumes such importance that it supplants the structured economy, economic development becomes ficticious. This situation impedes economic development and was condemned by the President of the Federation of Congolese enterprises, Monsieur Yuma, when he publicly stated that approximately "16 billion dollars circulate within the country outside the banking system and divorced from the formal economy."[291]

This worrying situation highlights the extent of the inefficacity of State structures. Currently the tax revenues of the Congolese State amount to 2.8 billion USD[292]; only a modest proportion of the potential tax receipts. With a modest reorganisation of its administration, in the current economic climate, the State should be able to double its revenue simply by widening the tax net.

---

[291] *Le Potentiel* n° 4879 of 20 March 2010.
[292] See the State Budget for the tax year 2008.

Like a sleeping elephant, DRC should wake from its slumbers. There should be a wake-up call to each Congolese citizen. It would influence development throughout the Central African States, most notably in the sub-region of the Great Lakes and a large part of Africa. It is essential to stimulate this renaissance by banishing administrative practices that have dragged the country down into economic chaos over several decades.

The struggle for Congolese citizens is the same as that experienced by all human societies in search of dignity and prosperity. It is evident that at various times the objectives are different, depending on current circumstances. The country's history provides some illustrations. If in 1959, society was then preoccupied by the inequalities created by the colonial system, itself based on a certain number of negative values, it is not far from the truth to say that, in 1992, post-independence society succeeded through a national conference to highlight the different points of view which legitimised the struggle for democracy. So that if a society like Congo does not reform itself on the basis of universal values, the victories that it imagines it has won are illusory and insubstantial in the light of history.

Moreover, this reflection is relevant to the actual situation in DRC, in a post-election climate with institutions created by popular demand. After the election in 2006, many were happy to make a linear evaluation. But it must be clear that dignity and prosperity are also important parameters in evaluating society. The Congolese have certainly won some battles in the context of democratic liberties and therefore acquired some dignity but, without economic prosperity, society regresses and the gains become burdens difficult to manage.

It is essential to start a real State reform. It is the number one priority. This overhaul should aim to allow the State to recover its sovereign functions. It is obvious, that in a State, which does not control national life, all effort is in vain. If the informal market in a State grows daily and anonymous individuals dictate to the State's legitimate institutional representatives the way the State is to be governed, the achievement of national interests is simply illusory.

The perspective of restructuring the State should include action to banish from the State apparatus all practices which attempt to privatise public activities. In so doing, respect for the law must be enforced, a law formulated with respect for fundamental human rights.

At economic level, it will be necessary to base the economic policy of the country on its resources and on the existing needs of the planet for which DRC can offer some solutions.

Moreover, it is essential to re-establish without delay disciplinary measures against the abovementioned negative values. This priority undertaking cannot be postponed.

We Africans, have until now provided solutions, without being consulted, to the problems of others. When America needed labour to work in the plantations in the south, we were the victims of slavery for 400 years. The resulting riches profited European economies and at the same time launched the booming American economy.

When it was necessary for Europe to find raw materials, a vast programme of colonisation kept our countries as externally managed economies for almost 100 years. A poorly negotiated decolonisation quickly plunged Africa into a difficult situation, forcing it to take positions not only contingent on its own interests but also relative to the Cold War.

Globalisation provides an opportunity for DRC and all of Africa to be aware of the need to make changes to have more weight in international exchanges. If not, following the example of what happened during slavery, colonisation and the Cold War, Africans risk remaining simple subjects serving the interests of others. It's now or never that decolonisation must come to an end.

# General Conclusions

Preceding arguments have indicated or tried to make a profound analysis of the need to make the countries surrounding the Atlantic, including those on the African coast, a new world development region, given the existing and historic relationships between peoples in this part of the globe.

First there was the desire to build Europe using black labour from Africa to clear the virgin lands of America, land destined for the production of riches for the old continent.

In its turn, the new continent profited from the immigration of Europeans to North America to boost growth in the developed world, and impose itself as the driving force for the entire world economy, after the Second World War.

More discreetly, Asia has become a major force for economic development; at first there was swift growth in Japan and then in China and India. However, even before the economic emergence of these last two nations there was rapid growth in a number of smaller Asian nations, especially Korea, Thailand, Malaysia and Singapore. These countries were commonly classed together under the label "Asian dragons". More recently, Vietnam has been added to the list of Asian nations experiencing strong economic growth.

Meanwhile, Latin America with Brazil in the lead is showing obvious signs of moving out of underdevelopment. The economy in this region then had a boost, when in addition to Brazil, countries like Venezuela, through its oil industry, and Chile (with its long term economic growth) arrived on the international scene.

Now there only remains Africa, or more precisely Sub-Saharan Africa which, with the exception of South Africa, continues to experience under-development categorised as "chronic".

Today, the black continent has the capacity to escape under-development like other parts of the world. Africa has, as does DRC, the full potential to respond to the opportunities of development and globalisation. But to succeed it is essential to make choices and be in the position to provide the wellbeing so heartily desired by local populations.

Obviously, the purpose of this work is to underline the ability of DRC to play its role based on its geopolitical situation; but it also has a modest ambition to stimulate an important group of countries favourable to DRC in this period of major world arbitration. This is a collective responsibility for all Congolese citizens.

This responsibility entails an obligation to act towards the objective, of creating a culture to correspond to the profound collective aspirations of Congolese citizens. Our country has a duty to offer its children a solid base and hope for the future. Hope to see unlimited horizons in our imagination and to transport us to the fulfilment of our dreams. This vision enables us to understand our ancestors and to learn from them[293], as we are now taking a risk with learning from Brazil's example.

Nobody has the right to renounce or make its people renounce the dream of a better world. Dreams are the inspiration for great achievements. Momentary difficulties cannot destroy the strength of our creativity. If men have been found wanting in their responsibility, it is up to them to relight the flame of hope through a responsible speech, a realistic project for society and the will to make a clean break. The miracle is human-based and it is in power of men of conscience to perform this painstaking action. We must not despair of the future, for it will be just as we will have decided here and now. The fruits of our action are the results of our thoughts.

DRC will be what we, Congolese people, will have decided, whatever that may be. We are under obligation to bequeath to future generations a more just, more prosperous and more humane society. This is a fundamental task which must find its impetus in the Congolese man of politics. He has to demonstrate his patriotism by guaranteeing equality of opportunity to each citizen.

Ten years, for me means two legislatures, a period in which to give the people the possibility of acquiring institutions, renewing them and especially to advance the democratic process.

Ten years, is the time-span given to the government to work flat out to ensure economic growth, with the help of massive investment in the

---

[293] See also KAMERHE, V., *"Repenser l'Atlantique"*, conference on 17 February 2010, University of Quebec in Montreal, Canada.

two fundamental sectors, namely social infrastructure and agriculture. After trying everything else, we now have the opportunity to get back to basics, i.e. with the economy serving man. And without hesitation, we say that the land is the way. A multi-sector approach to agriculture will set free creative energy and give us the basis for an acceptable development.

Ten years also means an opportunity to programme real sectoral policies, based on strategies to combat social inequality.

Ten years is the time to ensure that basic education is free for our children.

Ten years is to provide good food for each mouth, water and electricity guaranteed for every home.

Ten years is also the time-span during which it is possible to give every Congolese family a decent environment. This is not a dream; it is a choice that the country has the means to achieve.

Finally, ten years is the time for a fresh chance that the country must grasp to make its mark in history.

Like Brazil, DRC is able to rise to these challenges which can be summarised as the fight against poverty.

This sad appeal is more than a profession of faith. It is made to men and women. Yes, growth, development and prosperity for everybody are possible. The commemoration of 50 years of independence on 30 June 2010 should have been a fitting occasion to have fresh thoughts about the administration of DRC, in order to make it a land of hope for the Congolese and all the people in the world.

Like Lula's Brazil, DRC has all the natural advantages, we were going to say, natural resources, to respond to the five great challenges that humanity is facing today: global warming, the food crisis, energy crisis, freshwater crisis and the crisis in raw materials.

The reorganisation of the Atlantic Region is an opportunity for DRC which should not only demonstrate its merits but also allow it to extract the maximum of advantages, but this first depends on the Congolese.

Combining market forces with a strong State can give fresh impetus to the economy to ensure sustained growth, taking social needs into account. But to do this, it is essential to set off with conviction on the road to good governance, which should not make the struggle against corruption and impunity merely a slogan. Clear leadership is necessary, which acts to progressively endow the State with the essential means to carry out its sovereign functions, justice, diplomacy, security and defence, and a fiscal and monetary policy oriented towards development. Finally it is necessary to work towards the reduction of social divisions and to consolidate peace.

This internal endeavour by each State will be accompanied by international co-operation and solidarity based on the "win-win" principle.

Africa, separated from America by the Atlantic or alternatively joined to America by the Atlantic, is leading a merciless combat against poverty and ignorance. In so doing, it is shouldering, from the point of view of ecological challenges, a large part of the burdens of humanity, of which Africa is the cradle, according to the eminent historians: Cheik Anta Diop and Joseph Kizerbo.

This is why the bridge worth placing between the two sides (of the Atlantic) is based not only on strategic interests but also on the premise of the uniqueness of the human race and the tactical obligation to solve future problems by participating in the search for solutions to current problems with neighbouring countries.

The Transatlantic Region and the world beyond form a whole where the striking advances of some and the deplorable backwardness of others constitute according to circumstances a stimulus for some and a burden for others.

Human destiny is interlinked so much so that if some countries advance without others there is a risk of creating other, often recurrent problems.

The countries of the North are confronted by a serious problem of clandestine immigration caused by the poverty of countries of the South. The solution is to create employment through investment and technology transfer to occupy the young in their own countries in the Southern Hemisphere, to increase the availability of basic social services and in short to reduce poverty

It is obvious that the States of the South have their role in this struggle for revival for a world imbued with justice and peace. Good governance with its integrated struggle against the cohorts of negative values, especially corruption, impunity, nepotism and the massive violation of human rights is the essential ingredient in social levelling for this part of the world and especially in Africa.

The black continent must stop being just a reservoir for raw materials and develop its own reprocessing industry, create its own internal market served not only by goods and services coming from elsewhere, but also from its own production with the excess perhaps being exported in a more elaborate and competitive form.

DRC should become a focus for integration in Central Africa like Nigeria is in Western Africa and the South African Republic in southern Africa. It is a role that the country played during the Cold War but from which it derived no benefit, probably because of the ambitions of its leaders at that time: to stay in power for their lifetime, and despite the opportunities, relegating the country's development to a secondary consideration.

At this time of globalisation the nation's ambitions should be re-evaluated to put them in line with its capacity as a contributor and its place in the world market. In this context, the first step is a realisation of the country's worth in terms of demographics, geopolitics, geostrategic and economic considerations, but only in terms of its potential for this last factor.

The State's overhaul of its sovereign functions, the symbiosis between political decision-makers and experts in science and technology, democracy as the administrative method for cities and consideration for the needs of urban, suburban and rural populations, all based on social justice built around equality and morality are the compulsory route to being accepted as credible, respectable and, why not, a permanent fixture on the world stage. This is what we describe as the "Sacred Union of Congolese Intelligence".

This Sacred Union is viewed as a tool to overhaul mental attitudes for the revival of the nation including the participation of all social classes in this task of national reformation, from university professors to female peasants in rural areas, not forgetting the market gardeners in the hinterlands around our cities.

DRC, our country, needs to give, and can give to the world and should give to humanity what it has received from nature and from history. It is only looking for points of contact and an arena for dialogue for a mutually fruitful and advantageous exchange of views. Transatlantic relations can be the lever for the increasing importance of co-operation where common sense has triumphed.

It is in this perspective that we proposed the creation of the Tricontinental Atlantic Conference, an excellent opportunity for a meeting to give and take for all nations around the Atlantic Ocean, in a spirit of complementarity, solidarity and justice.

# strada lex

## L'accès le plus direct à toute l'information juridique
## www.stradalex.com

Je ne suis pas encore abonné à Strada lex et je désire connaître
les conditions qui me permettront de consulter en ligne
les monographies Larcier que j'aurai acquises

☐ Je demande à recevoir le passage d'un délégué de votre maison d'édition
de préférence à l'une des dates suivantes :

_____

_____

✓ Lors de son passage, le délégué me fera une démonstration des
fonctionnalités de Strada lex
✓ Lors de son passage, le délégué me communiquera le prix et les
conditions générales de l'abonnement à Strada lex

Je, soussigné(e),

Nom _____ Prénom_____

Société _____

N° TVA _____

Profession _____

Rue _____ N° _____

CP _____ Localité _____

Adresse e-mail _____

Signature                      Date

FOTRADRC-58362- CDU3481

Nous vous remercions de compléter le formulaire ci-dessus et de nous le
retourner par courrier, fax ou courriel à l'adresse ou au numéro ci-dessous :

**Groupe De Boeck s.a.**
**Éditions Larcier**
Fond Jean-Pâques 4 • 1348 Louvain-la-Neuve
Tél. +32 (0)2 548 07 20 • Fax +32 (0)2 548 07 22 • info@stradalex.com
**www.larcier.com**